THE PICTURE GUIDES

❀

THE ARDENNES

AND

THE WALLOON COUNTRY

Published in French by B. ARTHAUD, Editions J. REY
GRENOBLE

THE ARDENNES
AND THE WALLOON COUNTRY

by CLIVE HOLLAND
Author of " Flanders & Hainault "

THE MEDICI SOCIETY
LONDON AND BOSTON

CONTENTS

914.93

Printed in France

To

H. M. Queen Elizabeth of Belgium,

this Book is

with Her Gracious Permission

respectfully dedicated

by

the Author.

London, Dec. 1927.

Liége. The Steps to the Citadel.

Antwerp. Landing Stages and Steen.

CHAPTER I

—

Antwerp, its churches, art treasures, ancient buildings and the Plantin Museum

As one comes up the broad and shallow Scheldt from the North Sea to Antwerp one passes at first through a wide estuary, with the Dutch islands of Walcheren and South Beveland to the north and that strange slice of what geographically speaking should by rights be Belgium, but which is actually a part of Holland, to the south. Then one enters a narrower but still wide river running south-eastward, with flat fields on either side; and in time comes to the great port, the prosperity of which has had so much to do with Belgium's high commercial position among the nations.

If one is fortunate one comes to Antwerp at sunset, for then the

Antwerp. View across the Scheldt.

Scheldt, with its low-lying shores, busy with traffic and ships of all kinds from the ocean-going liner, pleasure steamers, and yachts to Belgian trawlers and quaintly shaped, bluff-bowed Dutch mussel boats and ferry boats passing from shore to shore, is, indeed, beautiful in its wide expanses of greyish-golden water, and the quiet of its landscape, beloved of Dutch painters, and often mysterious and wonderful with cloud effects, and a sense of atmosphere in the fading light.

Right ahead, as the steamer draws in towards the outskirts of the city, one catches glimpses of a mass of red and slate grey roofs, and here and there ancient buildings sandwiched in between modern offices; and a jumble of vast warehouses in which lie stored the produce, treasures of all nations, borne across the restless waters of the seven seas. And above all this expanse of picturesque roofs, with the skyline broken here and there by minaret-like towers and domes, rises the Gothic northern tower of the beautiful Cathedral soaring upwards 404 feet.

Not without reason did Charles V compare the exquisite and elaborate stone tracery of its tower to Mechlin lace.

Then, as the steamer passes slowly along the line of busy quays to its berth, the ancient Steen, originally a portion of the

Castle of Antwerp, dating from the tenth century comes into view.

What a sight are these docks and quays of Antwerp! Miles of them, alongside which great steamers are berthed, discharging their cargoes by means of huge cranes, and gangs of stevedores whose antlike movements fascinate the beholder; or taking in cargoes of manufactured articles for transport to the far off corners of the civilised and even uncivilised world.

Such is one's first view and impression of Antwerp, which, with its population of upwards of 400,000, including the suburbs of Berchem and Borgerhout, is, excepting Brussels with its fifteen self-governing suburban communes, the greatest city of Belgium, and was until the War considered second only to Metz as a fortress.

Antwerp and the Scheldt have been compared not inaptly with Liverpool and the Mersey. But the Scheldt — although at times visited by fogs as is the Mersey — on bright summer days has a picturesqueness and clarity of atmosphere that the latter river seldom enjoys, and the quays and wharves of Antwerp have characteristics which differentiate them from those of its English counterpart. Certainly Antwerp forms one of the most interesting of Belgian cities of to-day, and although year by

Antwerp. Vessel unloading.

year the growth of the suburbs serves more and more to dwarf the comparatively small element of medievalism still remaining, there are yet to be found not a few old corners and buildings, other than those known to all, of interest and architectural charm. If for no other reason than its possession of many masterpieces of the painters' art, the work

Antwerp. One of the Docks.

of Paul and Mathieu Bril, Rubens, the Van Dycks, Teniers, Quentin Matsys, B. Van Orley, Jordaens, Seghers, and others, who all in past times lived and worked here, Antwerp would have a great attraction for the student and all lovers of the art of painting, in which the city ranked so high during the seventeenth century, and even may be said to have then enjoyed a pre-eminence.

Antwerp may be truly called a Flemish city. Few things strike the student of character and social customs more forcibly in Antwerp than the Flemish sentiment, which is at once apparent when one becomes on intimate terms with the people. Flemish is the language generally spoken not only by the common folk, but by many people of the middle and upper middle classes, although, of course, the latter can,

The Scheldt. Looking across to the Tête de Flandre.

and do when necessary, speak French, which is the language of the greater commercial houses, and officially of the Government of the town.

Most visitors to Antwerp other than those drawn to it by business interests come to the city whose ancient walls were washed by the waters of the Scheldt, on account of its beautiful Cathedral of Notre-Dame, and its wonderful treasures of art. Antwerp, indeed, is proud of its historic Cathedral, which stands just beyond the north western corner of the picturesque tree - shadowed Place Verte, where in spring, summer and autumn one can always find a wealth of beautiful flowers

Antwerp. Along the Quay.

whose multitudinous tints add to it a gaiety and brightness, and whose fragrance perfumes the air.

Although this largest and perhaps most beautiful Gothic church in the Netherlands is known as the Cathedral, it no longer contains the seat of a bishop, but forms part of the diocese of Malines. Notwithstanding that it is an extremely fine example of Early and Middle Gothic architecture — the tower is Late Gothic or Flamboyant in style — it is possibly at first sight, at all events externally, somewhat disappointing. One reason for this is the fact that it is unfortunately shut in by many houses of quite a mean character. And thus the full beauty of the building is not seen from the Place Verte, which as an open space should naturally form a splendid approach to it. The spire has come in for a good deal of latter day criticism. We read in one author that it is " gingerbread-like and meretricious "; and in another that it is " overladen with ornament, and looks cheap and tawdry ". Neither one nor the other criticism we have quoted will, we fancy, be accepted as final or as just by those for whom Late Gothic architecture, with its beauty of tracery and ornament, possesses a greater attraction than the earlier and severer forms of Gothic school.

The most conspicuous portion of the exterior, other than the spire,

Antwerp. Entrance to the Steen.

Antwerp. The Steen anciently the Castle of Antwerp.

seen from the Place Verte, is the beautiful portal, which has been of recent years extensively restored, and the south transept. There is little sculpture on them with the exception of a small figure of the Virgin with the Child placed high up in the gable end. To see the west front one must go round into the little Marché aux Gants, whence one has a view of the fine central portal and the west window, flanked by the two great towers, the southernmost of which unhappily was left unfinished, and is consequently very dwarfed in appearance. The northern side of the Cathedral, it must be admitted, has been rather over much restored.

The building is cruciform in shape with triple aisles and ambulatory, and is generally supposed to have been begun in the year 1352 under the direction of Jean Amel or Appelmans a native of Boulogne, his son, Peter continuing the work after his death in 1398. In 1434 a new mind — that of Jean Tak — was brought to bear upon the structure, and only a few years later, in 1449, one Master Everaert took over the superintendence of the great work. To this period — that is to say from the middle of the fourteenth till the middle of the fifteenth century — the choir with its ambulatory and chapel, the sacristies, and the tower as far up

Antwerp. The Corner of the Quai Van Dyck.

as the first gallery belong. The aisles were built during the period covered by the first quarter of the fifteenth to the beginning of the sixteenth century, when the building operations were under the direction of Herman de Waghemaker and his son Dominic. To them also are generally ascribed the dome above the crossing, and the late Gothic of the upper portion of the northern tower, the final pinnacle of which was probably added about 1592. The work upon the southern tower was abandoned in 1474 when it had reached only about a third of its original contemplated height.

On entering the Cathedral the visitor cannot fail to be struck by its size, and impressiveness. The perspective of its six aisles affords a very charming vista, and on days of bright sunshine the beauty of the picture is largely enhanced by the light streaming in through the stained

Antwerp. The Flower Seller.

Antwerp. The Steen.

glass windows and falling in diaper pattern upon the flagstones beneath.
Although the work of building was extended over a period cover-
ing nearly two centuries, a general plan seems to have been adhered to

throughout
with some
degree of
closeness.
Thus the
whole pre-
sents a toler-
ably uniform
aspect, and
though its
parts differ
in detail they
are, notwith-
standing
this, homo-
geneous in
form.

Quite in-
dependently
of its great
size and im-
pressiveness
the Cathe-
dral, which
has an ex-
treme length
of 384 feet,
a width of
nave of 171
feet, of tran-
sept 212 feet,
and a height
of 130 feet,
is celebrated

Antwerp. Brabo Fountain and Guild Houses,
Grande Place.

from the fact that it has a nave of six aisles, three on either side, giving
to it an extremely striking appearance. One feature that immediately
arrests one on entry is the absence of a choir screen in a country where

Antwerp. Hôtel de Ville.

screens of a lofty character are most frequent, but the absence adds much to the beauty of the interior.

The absence of a triforium and the consequent proximity of the arcade and clerestory gives a rather modern and non-Gothic touch to the nave as it stretches out before one.

The chief defect of the Cathedral is the frequent and monotonous repetition of parts and details, that marks the decay of the spirit of Gothic architecture and design which had come about when the church was erected.

The choir stalls, filling the first two bays on either side were placed there as recently as the middle of the last century. In 1860 the stalls were finished by the famous Louvain sculptor Karel Hendrik Geerts, and his elaborate and beautifully carved groups and statues should on no

Antwerp. Calvary of la Vieille Boucherie.

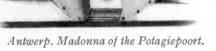

Antwerp. Madonna of the Potagiepoort.

account be overlooked by the lover or student of good carving. The beautiful and imaginative handiwork of Geerts has done much to remove the impression of poverty and bareness which the stall work originally gave. And this is now one of the most splendid examples to be met with of the revival of Medieval art.

The great artistic treasures, however, of the Cathedral are the works of Rubens. The high altar piece is enriched by that triumph of his genius, " The Assumption ", painted in 1626, and of all the creations of the artist perhaps there is none other which more thoroughly exhibits his great grasp of religious decorative art. It is certainly one of the best of the ten pictures the Master painted, all having the same subject, none of which it is interesting to note, except this one, is placed where the artist originally intended. The work, of course, is seen at a considerable distance, but every outline of the picture is instinct with light, so that the central figure of the Virgin is seen ascending in dazzling glory. The Virgin is caught up into the air by a circle of little cherubs, whilst below stand the Apostles gazing into the empty tomb, and the centre of the foreground is occupied by the Holy Women about to pluck roses.

On the left wall of the south transept is hung Rubens' great triptych known as " The Descent from the Cross ".

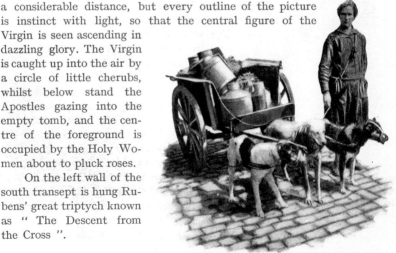

Antwerp. A dog-drawn milk-cart.

Antwerp. The Cathedral Tower.

The story of the picture is that Rubens agreed to paint the Guild of the Arquebusiers a picture of St. Christopher, the Patron Saint of the Guild, to settle a dispute regarding the cost of a wall which separated the garden of his studio from some land belonging to the Guild. The artist did it after his most magnificent fashion, and illustrated the subject in four ways by this famous triptych, and the picture on its exterior. In the pictures within the shutters, on the left hand, Mary is seen in the subject of the Visitation; the central picture is the Descent from the Cross, with the dead Christ borne by Joseph of Arimathea and the Disciples; and the right hand panel shows the Presentation in the Temple, where the living Christ is borne in the arms of Simeon.

The picture was placed in position in 1612, and forms the greatest treasure of the Cathedral. The outer shutters of the work are seldom seen now-a-days although the sacristan will usually disclose them on request, when the figure of St. Christopher, and the Hermit with his owl and lantern directing the saint to Christ is seen.

In the second chapel of the Ambulatory is the tomb of Jan Moretus, son-in-law of Plantin, with pictures painted by Rubens, who was a friend of the famous printer.

Many of the chapels contain fine altar pieces generally modern, but of archaic design. In the north transept on the right wall is found Rubens' " Elevation of the Cross ", painted in 1610 for the High Altar of Ste. Walburge. This was the artist's first great work after his return from Italy, and for it he received the then large sum of 2600 florins. The picture is in the form of a triptych, but the main idea continues

Antwerp. Statue of Rubens, Place Verte.

through the three panels. Although this work exhibits, when seen in a strong light, some of the most individual features of the artist's style, it cannot be said that he reached in it the highest attainment of sacred art.

Fine as the Cathedral is, and interesting to architectural students, the interior leaves on one rather the impression of vastness than of actual beauty, and the most enduring memories of it will undoubtedly be the works of Rubens, although there are other interesting pictures by lesser masters.

On leaving the building one should pause for a moment in the Marché aux Gants to see the ancient well with its charming Gothic canopy, and statuette of Salvius Brabo, which is generally supposed to be the work of Quentin Matsys. Near by is the birthplace of David Teniers the younger.

Antwerp. The Old meat market.

Antwerp possesses several other fine and interesting churches, and those of St. Jacques, and St. Paul should certainly be visited. The former is readily reached on foot from the Cathedral by way of the Marché au Lait along the Courte Rue Neuve and the Longue Rue Neuve; about mid-way down the latter, at the corner of the Rue St. Jacques stands the church.

It is cruciform in plan and well-proportioned, but unfortunately

suffers, as does the Cathedral itself, from its environment. It is an interesting building in the style of the later period of the Pointed; that is to say from about 1479-1505, and is distinguished by the great simplicity of its arrangement and details. It contains many works of sculpture of great merit by various distinguished Flemish artists.

One might almost call St. Jacques the Westminster Abbey of Antwerp on account of the number of the wealthiest and most distinguished families of the city who have for centuries been buried within its walls. One of the most interesting Chapels in the ambulatory is that of the Rubens family, containing the vault where he is buried. The

Antwerp.
The Old meat market.

altar was presented by his widow in 1642, and on it is a picture by Rubens representing the Virgin, Infant Christ, and Saints, one of the last of his works. An added interest is given to the latter from the fact that the face of St. George is generally supposed to have been painted by Rubens from his own countenance, while his two wives appear in the persons of Mary Magdalene and Martha, and his

Antwerp. An Ancient Street.

father is reproduced as St. Jerome, his son as one of the hovering cherubs, and his aged grandfather as the figure of Time.

In the pavement of the Chapel is his tombstone, with his armorial bearings — a hunting horn, to which he added in succession the two roses of Spain, the leopard of England, and the fleur de lys of France. There is also in St. Jacques some good stained glass, most of it dating from the seventeenth century.

The choir stalls of the same period should also not be missed as they were carved by the Elder and Younger Quellin, and still bear the arms of the noble families to which they once belonged. Rubens' stall is the twelfth to the left from the entrance.

The Confessionals of St. Jacques in the Ambulatory, on the south side along the walls of the choir, are famous almost all over the world. They are

Antwerp. Statue of Rubens.

the work of Artis Quellin the elder, Louis Willemsens his pupil and other noted wood carvers of the middle half of the seventeenth century.

The church of St. Paul is near the Marché au Bétail, and stands in a picturesque part of the city. It is most easily and best reached by way of the quays.

The church was formerly that of the adjoining Dominican monastery, and is in the Late Gothic style prevalent during the period of its erection 1533-1571. Over the outer doorway of the court is a fine relief depicting St. Dominic receiving the Rosary from Our Lady, and to the right, as one enters the church, is a gaudy Calvary constructed of rock and rubble erected against the wall of the transept. Above it is the Crucifixion, below the Entombment and the Holy Sepulchre, whilst all round are other scenes including St. Peter with the Crowing Cock, Christ and the Magdalene in the Garden, with a number of statues of saints, angels, prophets and others. It is a poor introduction to a very beautiful church, on entering which, one is at once struck by its elegant and fine proportions, and it should certainly be visited by all students of architecture if only because it presents one of the best examples of the more refined type of church built in Belgium by the Dominican Order. It should be noted, however, that the choir, which was not completed till 1621 differs considerably in style from the nave. As in the Church of St. Jacques, the Confessionals are adorned with good eighteenth century wood carvings including life size figures. Over the altars in the south transept is the picture of the Disputation on the Blessed Sacrament, painted by Rubens immediately after his return from Italy, and a picture by the elder Teniers, depicting the Seven Works of Mercy. The north transept contains another Rubens " The Scourging of Christ " ; and in the north aisle are the mysteries of the Rosary, fifteen paintings by various artists dating from the early years of the seventeenth century.

Antwerp. Quentin Matsys Well.

Antwerp. Façade of the Cathedral.

Antwerp.
Window in St. Jacques.

One should not miss a tiny enclosed square called the Potagie Poort, reached from No. 15 Place St. Paul, which is one of the most quaint and delightful portions of ancient Antwerp.

After its Cathedral it is generally on account of its Art collections that Antwerp presents the greatest attraction for visitors. The handsome picture gallery in the Place Leopold de Wael, known as the Musée des Beaux-Arts, has many works of art of the greatest interest and value, representing the various phases of the development of the Flemish school, and examples of other Continental masters. The Rubens collection, which is the great glory of the museum, founded in 1877 by the city of Antwerp and the Belgian State, is housed on the ground floor of the right wing of the building, with an overflow into an ante-room. The collection contains about 2000 reproductions, engravings, etchings, wood cuts, photographs, etc. of most of the existing works of Rubens, and for the student is of the utmost value in that it gives an insight into the wonderful versatility and inexhaustible powers of the great artist There are, also, of course, quite a number of Rubens pictures including "The Adoration of the Magi", painted in 1624; "Christ Crucified Between the Two Thieves", painted for the Church of the Franciscans four years earlier; "Christ à la Paille", a picture representing the body of Christ upon a stone bench

Antwerp. Church of St. Paul.

covered with straw; and a most interesting altar piece, painted about 1617, with the Virgin and Child and St. John the Evangelist upon the wings.

Rubens was one of the most prolific of masters, and may be said to have been a genius at " lightning " studies, although many of the pictures which occupied him scarcely as many days as they might have taken weeks, show very little trace of the extraordinary rapidity with which he worked. Not a few of his largest canvasses, it is said, were done in a fortnight.

In the Hall of the Ancient Masters of the Antwerp Museum, one finds

Antwerp. Famous Confessionals
Church of St. Jacques.

examples both of native and foreign art, and among them many pictures well worth the study not only of students but of all in the least interested in the evolution of an art. In the magnificent collections gathered beneath

Antwerp. Memlinc. Christ as King of Heaven (detail).

the roof of this fine building are examples of Quentin Matsys, David Teniers, Michel Coxie, B. Van Orley, Maerten de Vos, Gerard Terburg, Franz Hals, Frans de Vriendt, Titian, Hobbema, Jacques Jordaens, Hans Memlinc, Jan Gossaert, and Hans Holbein to mention only the more important.

The ancient centre of Antwerp was the Grande Place, and it is in the immediate neighbourhood of this, and the Cathedral that one naturally wanders amid narrow, winding streets and alleys in search of survivals of the once numerous houses of the merchant princes of the past. Most of the old Guild Houses, formerly belonging to the different corporations, were erected in the sixteenth and seventeenth centuries. One of the oldest of these is the Maison des Tonneliers (House of the Coopers) built in 1579 restored half-a-century later and at various periods since. Another fine example is the five storeyed Maison de la Vieille Arbalète or Oude

Voetboog built in 1516 largely reconstructed in 1580, with a double

Antwerp. Rubens. The Descent from the Cross.

storeyed gable surmounted by a gilded figure of St. George on horseback.
On the south eastern side of the Grande Place are the Maison des Drapiers

(House of the Clothiers) and Maison des Charpentiers (the Hall of the Carpenters) both of which date from the early days of the fifteenth century, but were rebuilt in 1542 and 1644. In No. 4 Grande Place was born Anthony Van Dyck in 1599.

On the western side of the Grande Place stands the fine Hôtel de Ville in the Renaissance style built in 1561-65 from designs by Cornelius de Vriendt. It was partially destroyed by the Spaniards, and rebuilt in its present form in 1581. It is a delightful building with an imposing façade 256 feet in length and 101 feet in height, with Doric and Ionic arcades in the two principal storeys. The central portion, with its circular arched windows, rises to a height of 183 feet in three additional storeys diminishing in size as they ascend. In a niche above, stands a figure of the Virgin as the tutelary saint of the city, which was placed in position in 1585, with allegorical figures of Wisdom and Justice on the right and left below. From just outside the Hôtel de Ville one gets one of the best views of the Cathedral.

Near the centre of the Grande Place is the famous Brabo fountain erected in 1887 from the design of Jef Lambeaux. Placed upon the pedestal of irregular rocks, the fine fountain is surmounted by a statue of Salvius Brabo, the mythical hero who defeated and cut off the hand of the legendary giant Antigonus, who used to exact a heavy toll from all the vessels entering the Scheldt, and in the event of a ship master refusing to pay cut off his right hand, and cast it into the river.

The Hôtel de Ville contains some interesting historical pictures and most of the rooms have good carved wooden panelling. There are several interesting and elaborate Renaissance chimney pieces, one of the most beautiful being that in the Burgomaster's room, originally in the old Abbey of Tongerlo. The chief subject of the carving is " The Last Supper ", above which are the " Raising of the Serpent in the Wilderness ", " The Crucifixion ", and " Abraham's Sacrifice ".

There are many interesting buildings still surviving in Antwerp, but among them none more beautifully preserved than the famous Musée Plantin-Moretus, standing in a corner of the little Marché du Vendredi, and reached pleasantly along the Quais Van Dyck and Plantin by the waterside, and Promenades.

The visitor to this ancient building will at once realise, as he enters it, that he has stepped into a different age, the noises of modern Antwerp and its streets, indeed, seem to be cut off, and within a totally different atmosphere prevails. The Museum derives its name from the famous printers Christopher Plantin and his son-in-law Jan Moretus. The house in which seven generations of the family of Moretus had carried on their business of printers, was acquired by the city of Antwerp in 1875.

The building is one of the most interesting and delightful in Belgium, as it remains essentially as it was when occupied by the famous printer

Antwerp. Rubens. The Entombment of Christ.

in the sixteenth century, an admirable example of the dwelling houses and business offices of wealthy and cultured Flemish citizen-merchants of that period. In this beautiful home, to enter which is to understand in some measure at least the graciousness and tranquility of past ages, are a number of early works by Rubens — 15 in all, and other interesting portraits and pictures by Antwerp and Flemish painters, fine tapestry, a spinet, old furniture, MSS. from ninth to sixteenth centuries, letters and documents relating to the families of Plantin and Moretus, and

Antwerp. Rubens. The Holy Family.

specimens of the books of the famous Plantin press. These latter include the celebrated " Biblia Polyglotta" published from 1568-73.

The printing office, reached across a beautiful courtyard, over the hoary walls of which rambles a wonderful old vine, is of great interest by reason of the fact that the various rooms remain in their original state, as though the workmen had but just left them after putting down the work upon which they had been engaged, to return very shortly and resume their labours. The ancient proof sheets are still lying about in the chamber formerly occupied by the proof readers; and in the type room the old matrices, formes, rules, and chases are still as they were left; and in the composing and printing rooms are two sixteenth century presses. The proprietor's room, and the chamber which it is traditionally believed the famous Professor Justus Lipsius, of Louvain University, used to occupy when on business visits to his publisher, Moretus, are equally interesting as giving one a clear and fascinating glimpse of a bygone age, and a knowledge of ancient things. The missals

Antwerp. Detail of Stall in St. Jacques.

and medieval MSS. preserved amid such admirable surroundings are worthy of close inspection and study, and the beautiful cabinets of mother of pearl and tortoiseshell are not likely to escape the notice of admirers and collectors of old furniture.

Among the many other notable and interesting buildings remaining in Antwerp one may mention the Bourse, most easily reached from the Place de Meir, which lies to the north east of the well-known Place Verte in the centre of which is the fine bronze statue to Rubens by W. Geefs. The Bourse or Exchange was erected in 1868-72 on the site

Antwerp. Rubens. The Adoration of the Magi.

of a fine late Gothic building by Dominic de Waghemaker dating from 1531, which was the oldest Exchange in Europe, and was burned down fifty years after its erection, and again in 1858. The present Bourse, designed by Joseph Schadde is in the same style as the original, but

Antwerp. Courtyard of Musée Plantin-Moretus.

upon a much larger scale with an entrance on each of its four sides. The fine Hall, which has a glass roof, is 56 yards long and 44 yards wide, and is surrounded by a double arcade with 68 columns all of different design, this opens towards the centre in Moorish-Gothic trefoil arches. Above these runs a gallery supported by columns, adjoining which is the Tribunal de Commerce, the walls adorned with the Arms of Antwerp and of different Provinces of Belgium. In the angles between the arches are those of the chief maritime nations. The building is used as a public thoroughfare except during business hours.

North eastward of the Bourse, most easily reached by the Place de Meir and Rue Jésus, is the magnificent national theatre the Flemish Opera House, a fine modern building standing facing the broad Avenue d'Italie (formerly Avenue de Commerce) the principal Flemish theatre in Antwerp. Among the other buildings of note in Antwerp one may mention the Palais de Justice reached by the fine Avenue de France (formerly Avenue des Arts) and Avenue Britannique (formerly Avenue de l'Industrie), a striking building erected from designs by Baeckelmans

Antwerp. The Colonnade of the Musée Plantin-Moretus.

Antwerp. Printing Room Musée Plantin-Moretus.

in 1871-5 and somewhat in the style of a French Château of Louis XIII.

A relic of the past well worth visiting and now devoted to the purposes of a War Museum is the Steen, situated midway along the Promenoirs or elevated Terraces which are thronged by Antwerp people on fine evenings, and afford extensive views of the busy shipping in the Scheldt, the great Fort de la Tête de Flandre, and the opposite shore.

The Steen, originally part of the Castle of Antwerp, through which the ascent to the Northern Promenoirs from the Quai Van Dyck now leads, dates from the tenth century, and remained in the hands of the lords of the soil till the middle of the sixteenth century, when Charles V made it over to the burghers of Antwerp. In addition to its many interesting War relics, including a wonderful collection of German placards, proclamations, and orders, with fragments of shells and bombs used in the siege of the city, there are collections of instruments of torture used by the Inquisition, furniture of the fifteenth to sixteenth centuries,

armour and weapons, glass manufactured in Antwerp of Venetian design, and some interesting costumes, ancient prints, engravings, and old views of Antwerp. There is also the head of the giant Antigonus by P. Coecke which has figured in all civic processions since the sixteenth century; and the head of the giantess by Herreyns dating from the eighteenth century.

After visiting the Steen it is worth while to stroll along the Quai Van Dyck to the Porte de l'Escaut or Watergate built in 1624 from designs by Rubens, and adorned with a seated figure of the river god by Artis Quellin the Elder.

Antwerp also possesses a good Jardin Botanique, and a famous Zoological Garden quite close to the Central Railway Station at the head of the fine Avenue de Keyser, considered one of the finest streets in Europe. The Zoo was founded in 1843 by the Société Royale de

Antwerp. Musée Plantin-Moretus. Seat support.

Zoologie, and is, with its restaurant, winter garden with palms and ferns, and Palais des Fêtes for concerts, etc., the favourite resort of the fashionable world in fine weather.

Antwerp offers to the enterprising searcher after ancient things and relics of former times a fairly prolific hunting ground, for here and there are to be discovered ancient and picturesque buildings, descriptions of which appear in no guide books, but are nevertheless for the student well worth discovery. The more modern portions of the town are distinguished by wide, well-kept, and pleasantly shaded boulevards, fine squares, and handsome

Antwerp. Musée Plantin-Moretus. Carved newel of staircase.

buildings so that Antwerp leaves upon the mind an impression of prosperity and of brightness.

One of the most beautiful natural features of the city are the gorgeous and wonderful sunsets which are so often seen across the Scheldt. Over the immense Fort de la Tête de Flandre, whose grimness is in such contrast to the roundabouts, swing boats, skittle alleys, and general air of enjoyment in the grounds of the Kursaal, on cloudy summer evenings there is a scene of aerial beauty scarcely equalled in any other part of northern Europe. On a " sunset " evening (as favourable atmospheric conditions are called) crowds throng the elevated Promenades by the waterside all intent upon the wonderful sky effects that the sun, wind, and atmosphere are, as it were, unrolling before them like some colossal cloud and seascape canvas by a great master.

Antwerp. Ferry across the Scheldt.

Lierre. The Nèthe.

CHAPTER II

—

Malines and its charm — Lierre — Louvain and its Hôtel de Ville and picturesqueness

Malines, which lies mid-way between Brussels and Antwerp is some fifteen miles distant from the latter by road. The country through which one passes is well cultivated but flat and not very interesting. It is not long before one catches sight of the great tower of the cathedral Church of St. Rombold standing up, clear-cut against the sky, over a tangle of ancient and picturesque houses.

Malines, anciently known as Mechlinia, is situated on the tidal river Dyle which, flowing through the town, by reason of its many branches gives to portions of Malines an almost Bruges-like character. The life of the town is chiefly centred in the district near the railway station where there is an element of bustle and industrial life provided by extensive workshops, rendered necessary by the fact that Malines is the intersecting point of several important lines of railway. The rest of the town seems but a sleepy, old-world place, in the streets of which one meets with many ecclesiastics, and in the summer also with a great number of tourists.

We have wandered in most of the streets of Malines at various times, and undoubtedly the best way to realise its peaceful charm and picturesqueness is to proceed from the wide Place de la Station along the Rue Conscience to the Porte d'Egmont, and, by way of the Place of the same name, to cross the seemingly currentless Dyle, from the bridge spanning which one gets a charming view in either direction, and on the right hand of the dome of Notre-Dame d'Hanswyck. The Rue Breul, which is the chief commercial street of the town, takes us to the Grande Place, around which are grouped some charming sixteenth and seventeenth

Lierre. Hôtel de Ville.

century gabled houses, with the Ancient Cloth Hall, rebuilt at various times from 1320 onwards, somewhat on the lines of the one at Bruges.

The Hôtel de Ville, though commenced at the beginning of the fourteenth century, was so entirely remodelled and largely rebuilt in 1715 that it is no longer of any great architectural interest. The fine, though somewhat decayed Vieux Palais, anciently known as the Old Schepenhuis, is situated at the entrance to the Grande Place. It is a Gothic building dating from the latter years of the fourteenth century, was used as the House of the Bailiffs from 1474-1618, and became the seat of the great Council or High Court of Justice for the Netherlands, founded by Charles the Bold in 1473. This ancient building now contains the valuable municipal archives and the city library. Among the treasures of the former are the account books of the city from the year 1311.

The dominating building of the town,

Lierre. Church of St. Gommaire.

however, is the magnificent Cathedral dedicated to St. Rombold, who was one of the earliest Christian missionaries in the Low Countries and suffered martyrdom on or near the site of the church on June 24th 775. This saint, who was the successor of Bishop Walraf by the command of an angel visitant, gave sight to the blind, relieved men of the evil spirits possessing them, and, besides raising a young noble to life, did many other miraculous acts. The Saint met his death while reproving a man for his sins. The offender turned upon him, and striking him with a hoe inflicted a fatal injury. It was for this reason that a hoe became St. Rombold's emblem.

Lierre. A Pietà.

Lierre. A corner near the Béguinage.

About the commencement of the last century no fewer than twenty-five paintings of scenes in his life were discovered, coated over with whitewash, in one of the Ambulatory Chapels of the Cathedral.

The magnificent and unfinished late Gothic western tower, which dominates the Grande Place and in fact the city itself, is 319 feet high, was begun in 1452-1513, and was intended by its architect, Wautier Cooman, and its founders to have a spire which would have been the highest in Christendom — namely 550 feet, or more than 20 feet higher than that of Ulm.

One should note the great western entrance which perforates the vast mass of masonry constituting the base of the tower, in many ways the latter is the most remarkable in the whole of Belgium. Its structure is in two stages, and the spire, never completed, was intended to form a third. Even the materials for it were brought on to the ground, when in 1583 the work was stopped by the Prince of Orange, who caused the stones

Lierre.
The entrance to the Béguinage.

Lierre. Rood Loft in St. Gommaire.

which had been prepared for the spire to be taken to Holland and used in the building of the town of Willemstad. The two completed stages of the tower are divided by a parapet of pierced work, marking the place of the platform between the buttresses. A similar parapet crowns the second stage placed upon a cornice, and follows the form of the buttresses so as to constitute a very beautiful detail of the work. One at once notices that the windows have cusped and crocketted hood mouldings, and those of the lower storey are very deeply recessed. The wall above these is marked by blind tracery and mullions in the Perpendicular style, as is often the case in similar English buildings. The church is a cruciform structure 306 feet in length, with a nave 89 feet in height, and 40 feet in width, and this unusual loftiness is such that great as is the height of the tower, especially from some points of view, the latter seems by no means out of proportion to the rest of the church. Many portions of the building, including the tower, have been so carefully and skilfully restored that it is difficult to describe, and, in some cases, even to detect, with any degree of accuracy, where the original work ends and the new begins.

But it may be said that the church, as a whole dates from the fifteenth

Lierre. Altar in St. Gommaire.

century, and the richest part of the exterior is found at the east end, which was built from the year 1356 onwards to about the middle of the fifteenth century when the apse was completed in accordance with the original design. The chapels of the ambulatory or choir aisle, and those of the east end project considerably beyond the buttresses and do not merely fill up the space lying between them, as is the most common practice in Belgian churches; indeed, the whole part of this work is rather French in character, with deeply recessed windows, and crocketted pyramids with carved finials, above which appears the light and elegant parapet.

The pulpit is a notable, if too elaborate, example of

Lierre. Entrance to the Rue du Béguinage.

the wood carving of the early part of the eighteenth century. The chief incidents depicted are the Conversion of St. Norbert, the Temptation of Adam by Eve, and Christ on the Cross.

The great art treasure of the church is the altar piece by Van Dyck, which was originally painted for the High Altar of the Church of the Recollects. It is undoubtedly one of the finest works of the master, and was painted by him after his return from Italy. The subject is " The Crucifixion ", and a dead Saviour is seen upon the Cross between two thieves, who seem alive and suffering. St. Mary Magdalene is at the foot of the Cross, the artist having rendered her passionate grief very strikingly.

Among the other churches of Malines which call for special notice

Malines. Brussels Gate.

is that of St. Jean, a late Gothic structure with a well proportioned western tower, and an unusually picturesque silhouette. The interior is severe and somewhat uninteresting, as the circular columns in the nave have plain capitals, and there is no arcading between the arches and the clerestory windows, which are filled with Flamboyant tracery. The church however, possesses a large Altar piece with pictures by Rubens, which are considered by some authorities among the best examples of the painter's ecclesiastical works. The inside pictures are the " Adoration of the Magi ", " The Beheading of John the Baptist ", and " St. John the Evangelist in the Cauldron of Boiling Oil ". The subjects of the paintings on the outside of the wings are " The Baptism of Christ ", and " St. John on the Island of Patmos writing the Apocalypse ".

The church of St Catherine, which lies to the north west of St. Jean is a much more interesting building, and is in the early fifteenth century style. Its central tower rises only one storey above the roofs of the nave,

Malines. The Grande Place and Cathedral.

choir, and transepts. The choir roof, which is of slate, and square, has architectural interest from its resemblance to some of those seen on Sussex and Kent churches.

To reach the very fine church of Notre-Dame d'Hanswyck one has to cross the Dyle into the opposite quarter of the city. It is a finely proportioned Flamboyant building, erected during the period between the commencement and the end of the first half of the sixteenth century, and in many respects bears a striking resemblance to the Cathedral. The transepts date from the first half of the sixteenth century, and the apse was not finished until the middle of the seventeenth.

Rich as it is in churches Malines does not rely solely for architectural interest upon these, fine though they be, for there are quite a con-

Malines. A Corner of the Market Place.

siderable number of ancient domestic buildings still standing which are well worth seeing. Many of these are to be found stowed away in obscure corners of one or other of the almost deserted quays, or in by-streets leading from them. At the corner of the Rue des Vaches and Rue St. Jean, not far from the church of that name, is the fine old Hôtel de Busleyden, a Gothic building dating from the first years of the sixteenth century, formerly the residence of Canon Busleyden, afterwards the Mont de Piété, and now the Academy of Music. Note the gables, and the arcades of considerable beauty.

Malines. Pulpit in Cathedral.

It has been well restored, and contains a fine chimney piece, and some interesting frescoes of the early sixteenth century, attributed to Jacopo de' Barbari, the chief subjects of which are the Nuptials of Amphitrite, and Balthazar's Feast.

South of the church of St. Peter and St. Paul lies the Palais de

Justice near the Place St. Pierre. It is a picturesque and interesting building, formerly the Palace of Margaret of Austria, who acted as Regent for her nephew Charles V in the sixteenth century. From 1561-1609 it belonged to the Granvellas family; after which for more than 150 years it was the seat of the Great Council. The older portions of the building which are in the Late Gothic style, date from quite the commencement of the sixteenth century, and the façade, which was built from 1517-26 from designs by Guyot de Beauregard, is particularly interesting, as it is stated to be the earliest, and one of the best examples of the Renaissance in Belgium. One should certainly see the interior, as it contains some fine chimney pieces, as well as a few works of art of note.

The wanderer in Malines in search of the picturesque will meet with many surprises, and though the present writer has paid the old city a number of visits, quite recently he made discoveries of unsuspected beauties of architecture in the lesser known streets which serve to prove that it is difficult to exhaust the pictorial or historical interest of an ancient town.

Other less known buildings worth seeing may be discovered by taking the following route, having as a starting place the Grande Place. Crossing this to its south western corner and proceeding down the Bailles de Fer on the south the wayfarer comes first of all to the Maison des Archers, an interesting house, although only dating from about the middle of the eighteenth century. Near by there is a fine iron railing of middle sixteenth century work bordering the canal. The central bridge, or Grand Pont, over the Dyle, built in the thirteenth century, should now be crossed, when turning to the left, and proceeding along the Zoutwerf or Quai au Sel, one comes to several charming specimens of richly Decorated Renaissance houses. One of them known as In den Grooten Zalmn, which dates from 1530, is the House of the Salmon, the Guild House of the Fishmongers. This was restored in the middle of the nineteenth century, and possesses a very interesting façade and interior, the former having carved friezes, panelling, pilasters, and arcades, on which are sculptured sea gods and goddesses, fishes, and similar subjects. The so called Lepelear, a little further along beyond two rather tumble-down timber houses, has some exquisite details in the Franco-Flemish style.

In further exploration it is best and easiest to take one of the by-streets on the right hand and strike into the Rue Notre-Dame, and proceed north-westwards to reach the Marché aux Grains. Here is the Maison de la Grande Arbalette, or the Guild House of the Crossbowmen, dating from the sixteenth century, but with a façade erected at the beginning of the seventeenth. It is along the Rue Haute that one reaches the sole survivor of the twelve ancient city gates, the Porte de Bruxelles, two " pepper box " towers linked together by an archway. It has, however, lost

Malines. Guildhouse of the Crossbowmen.

much of its original character owing to having been rebuilt in the seventeenth century.

Malines. Church of St. John.

A pleasant way to reach the other quays along the Dyle, on which here and there interesting houses are still surviving, is to leave the Porte de Bruxelles, and proceed by the Rue Haute from which point one is able to reach the waterside again by one or other of the streets on the left. And walking along by the Dyle one comes to the Quai aux Avoines or Haverwerf, on which there are two interesting houses overlooking the now almost deserted waterway with its Venetian-like posts sticking up in the water to which anciently barges were moored.

Malines. View from tower of the Cathedral.

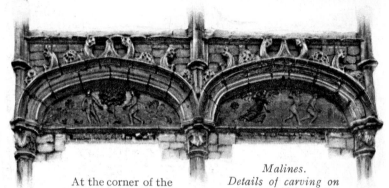

Malines.
Details of carving on
Maison du Paradis.

At the corner of the Rue de la Grue is the so called Paradise house, with its two painted reliefs of the Fall and Expulsion of Adam and Eve from Eden. Close by is the Maison des Diables, a fine timbered house of the sixteenth century, the front of which is embellished with quaint carvings. The pillars on either side of the door have boy statuettes holding a shield. On the sides of the windows of the first storey are carved satyrs, and on the mullions a faun, all grinning. On the second tier are a series of nine curious brackets placed between the windows and carved with grotesque figures of warriors, a king and a queen etc., whilst the verge board shows a seraph at each foot. Near by is another house on the front of which is a curious carving of God and Christ, and a date 1689 which refers to the upper part.

There is something very charming

Malines.
Detail of carving
on Maison des
Diables.

Malines. Doorway of Maison des Diables.

about the neighbourhood of these narrow waterways where many other buildings and fragments of Gothic and Renaissance houses and architec-ture may be found by the enterprising searcher. It may be truly said, we think, that scarcely any city in Belgium is so rich as Mali-nes in quaint buildings — Gothic, Re-naissance, and seven-teenth centu-ry houses.

Malines, has, of course, for centuries been celebra-ted for its ex-quisite lace. Some of the best of the ancient lace, which the skil-ful fingers of long dead *den-tellières* have produced, is almost price-less; and even that of to-day

Malines. Courtyard of the Palais de Justice.

is very beautiful and costly. In many of the houses of the quarter of the city lying north west of the Cathedral the *dentellières* still work at their beautiful and fascinating calling.

The impression one carries away of this picturesque and historic city is that of a town whose soul still lingers in the Middle Ages notwithstanding the occasional bustle of modern life caused by the incursion of large parties of tourists, the introduction of trams, and the carrying on of certain modern industries on the outskirts of the town.

Lierre which lies a few miles to the north east of Malines is a picturesque lace-making town of some 25,000 inhabitants at the confluence of the Grand and Petit Nèthe; which, although it suffered severely during the War, has yet much remaining of interest. Few of the ordinary travellers in Belgium seem to have discovered it, as, distant almost equally from Antwerp and Malines, it lies off the track and consequently its interests and glories are almost unknown to foreign tourists.

The town is very closely associated with one of the heroes of the Belgian Revolution Jenneval by name who was the composer of Belgium's National Anthem, the " Brabançonne ", for it was in the town that he met his death. He was born at Louvain, and his real name was Louis Dechez, he took the name Jenneval when he went on the stage. The " Brabançonne " caught the national spirit, and like the "Marseillaise" in France was sung from one end of the country to the other.

Malines. The Quai aux Avoines.

The chief treasure of Lierre is the church of St. Gommaire, one of the most interesting churches in Belgium in the Flamboyant style. The building was greatly favoured by the Emperor Maximillian, who presented to it three beautiful windows, which were quite uninjured at the time of the outbreak of War, but were badly damaged during the bombardment of the town. The church was commenced

Malines. Ancient Markets and Hôtel de Ville.

in 1425, and completed in 1557. It is considered one of the most perfect and interesting Late Gothic churches in Belgium, and part of the earlier church of the eighth century still remains in the shape of St. Peter's Chapel. The rood loft, which should be noted, dates from 1534, and is the work of Francis Mynsheeren and J. Wischavens of Malines. The altarpiece is twenty-four years earlier, and is the work of the artist known as the master of St. Catherine's Altar at Antwerp. The church possesses the two wings of a triptych ascribed to Rubens, the subject of one, which is in the south transept, is St. Francis, with a good landscape as the background; and the subject of the other, hanging in one of the Ambulatory chapels, is St. Clare. The reliquary of St. Gommaire is a fine specimen of the silversmith's art and dates from 1668.

It was in this church in October 1496 that Philip the Fair of Burgundy was married to the Infanta Joanna of Aragon and Castille by Henry de Berg, Bishop of Cambrai.

Not far from the church is an old mansion known as the Hof van Denemarken, or the Danish House. Here Christian II of Denmark, known as the Cruel, lived for some years, after his exile in 1524.

The old Belfry, which dates from 1369, has turrets on the four corners, and is linked on to the Hôtel de Ville, but the present building is only of the seventeenth century. In the Market Place are some curious and interesting old houses, with Renaissance façades.

The street of the Béguinage is entirely charming, and the peaceful rows of little cottages, some of which were alas! damaged during the War, always seem to tempt artists, for one seldom goes there without seeing some of the fraternity of the brush busily at work. There is a quaint central garden in the inner courtyard. It is said by some authorities that the Béguines owe their name and the institution of their Order to St. Begge, daughter of Pepin of Landen who resided at Lierre in a house called the Béguinage, originally just outside the walls of the town. Lierre Béguinage is one of the most ancient; there is a charming staircase in the vestibule which has a beamed ceiling.

In the Rue de Malines, a turning out of the Grande Place, is the Musée Wuyts van Campen of some considerable importance as it contains many local antiquities, and a cabinet of rare engravings. There is also a picture gallery in which are hung some interesting Flemish and Dutch paintings with examples of Rubens, Van Dyck, Teniers, etc. Like so many other Flemish towns Lierre has besides famous buildings many hidden treasures of architecture in its courts and lanes, lingering on untouched by the passage of time, with an atmosphere of bygone days to lend to them beauty and romance.

Louvain, which is almost equidistant from both Brussels and Malines, at the eastern apex of a triangle formed by the railway system, suffered more severely than most towns of its size in Belgium during the War, and sustained an irreparable loss by the destruction, through burning, of its University and world-famous Library. But this still interesting town situated on the Dyle, which flows through it and is connected by a canal with the Rupel, contains many buildings of importance including the beautiful Late Gothic Hôtel de Ville, rivalling that of Brussels and almost unnatural in its elaboration of detail, which happily escaped any

Louvain. Avenue des Alliés.

serious damage. Erected by Matthew de Layens in 1447-1463, in the centre of the town that had nearly three centuries before been encircled " by a strong wall upon which were forty towers ", it is said to have been commenced on the Thursday after Easter Day, and to have occupied fifteen years in building. This wonderfully ornate Town Hall — indeed, some critics are inclined to esteem this particular feature a defect — is a mass of turrets, pinnacles, statues, dormers, canopies, tracery, and quaint and delicate ornamentation.

The building consists of three lofty storeys, each of them containing ten pointed windows in the principal façade, surmounted by a steep roof surrounded by an open balustrade. Although architecturally so rich, it is one of the smallest buildings of its kind in any city of similar note and importance in the Low Countries. The façade is 108 feet long and 73 feet in height to the parapet with a width of 42 feet; and six slender and elegant octagonal turrets, crowned by graceful open spires, rise from the corners and spring from the centre of the gables, giving a dignity and richness to the elevation and silhouette of the building. The exterior was restored in 1828-41 when the statues in the niches between the windows were inserted; the bases of the niches are carved with Biblical subjects

some of them of a truly medieval grotesqueness and freedom of treatment. The western gable was seriously damaged by lightning in 1890, but waas afterwards restored. Unfortunately time and weather have found in the intricate and delicate tracery and carvings of this wonderful Hôtel de Ville a peculiarly sensitive material upon which to work destruction, and thus the restorations which have been undertaken at various times must have cost immense sums. The work as a whole must be admitted to have been well and carefully done, but of necessity some of the modern compares unfavourably in beauty with the old that in part it replaces, and is hard — a failing only time can remedy.

It would be difficult to describe in any detail the variety of the carvings upon the façades. In all there are no fewer than 280 niches for statues, which represent persons identified with, and prominent in, the history of Louvain. A veritable portrait gallery in stone.

The interior of the Hôtel de Ville does not correspond

Louvain.
War Memorial.

as regards antiquity with the exterior. Most of the apartments are furnished in modern style, and adorned with pictures by Otho Vaenius, de Crayer, Mierevelt, etc. On the second floor is a small picture gallery of old and modern paintings in which is a diptych by Jan Van Rillaert of Louvain.

Louvain possesses

On the road near Louvain.

Louvain. Hôtel de Ville.

Louvain. Window in Hôtel de Ville.

several good and interesting churches, and of these the Late Gothic and spireless building of St. Pierre, standing opposite the Hôtel de Ville on the Grande Place, is the most important. It was begun in about 1425 by Sulpice Van Vorst of Diest, who was succeeded by Jan Kelderman of Malines, in 1439, and by Layens in 1445. The towers of the western façade were begun by Joas Matsys in 1507, but were reduced in 1612-30 to the level of the roof on account of the foundations proving too weak to carry them.

The church is nearly 334 feet in length and about 82 in breadth, and of a like height. The interior is lighted by 90 windows with Flamboyant tracery. The nave contains an elaborate pulpit of the middle of the eighteenth century, and other works of art. The restored rood loft, which is very fine and elaborately carved dates from 1490. In the north transept is a wooden statue of the Virgin dating from 1441, known as the " Sedes sapientiae ", before which doctors of the University lay

Louvain.
Carving : Hôtel de Ville.

their confessions of faith. The fine Renaissance screen is by Jan Veldener, 1568. Other notable works are the old copy of Roger Van der Weyden's triptych " The Descent from the Cross " in the Prado at Madrid; in the tenth bay a triptych of " The Last Supper " by Dierick Bouts restored to Belgium by the Treaty of Versailles; and in the last ambulatory Chapel is the black marble tomb of Matilda of Flanders wife ot Duke Henry I, and ot her daughter Mary, died 1260, wife of the Emperor Conrad IV.

The famous tabernacle for the reception of the

Louvain. Church of St. Michael.

Reserved Sacrament, stands under the last arch on the north side of the choir. It forms one of the most wonderful and elaborate examples in Belgium, it is nearly 50 feet in height, and is literally a mass of crocketted pinnacles and ornamentation, upon which artists of the fifteenth century appear to have loved to expend time, thought and ingenuity. It was constructed from the designs of Matthew de Layens the architect of the Hotel de Ville.

The merely curious and those for whom legend and romance possess a fascination will look with interest upon the large black Byzantine Crucifix, placed in the south aisle, on which the figure of Christ wears an ancient red velvet robe, reaching to the feet embroidered with stars and tongues of gold. It is probably eleventh or twelfth century work, and

Louvain. Famous Altarpiece by Dierick Bouts.

is to this day greatly venerated by the common people because of the story which attaches to it. It is to the effect that a thief, who long ago broke into the church intent upon sacrilege, was seized by the figure and held fast until he was discovered by the sacristan of the church.

The Halles erected in 1317, as a warehouse for the wealthy and powerful Cloth Workers Guild, were in 1679 given up to the purposes of the University which had been founded in 1426. This, almost utterly destroyed by the Germans, has been rebuilt and where possible restored.

Though none of the churches in Louvain except that of St. Pierre is of any great note or importance, if time allows, the visitor will not have cause to regret an hour or two spent in visiting the church of St. Michael, which stands at the end of the Rue de Namur, and distant from the University only a few hundred yards; St. Gertrude, which lies in quite an opposite direction northward along the Rue de Malines, and stands close to the Porte of the same name; and the Dominican church of Notre-Dame close by. The first named church of St. Michael is chiefly interesting as a good, and perhaps, one might say one of the most striking, examples of the work of the architects who were responsible for the Belgian Baroque style. St. Gertrude, formerly the church of an Abbey, is an elegant and well pro-portioned building, unfortunately very much hemmed in by houses. The chief charm of the church to the ordinary visi-tor will undoubtedly be the famous and interesting choir stalls of which there are two ranks. They are the work of Ma-thias de Wayer, and date from 1550. The

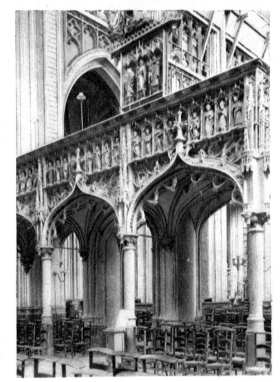

Louvain. Rood Screen, Church of St. Pierre.

carvings ornamenting the backs of the upper row of stalls depict scenes

Louvain. Detail of Rood Screen.

in the History of Religion, some of them curious, and of considerable antiquarian interest.

There is a fine Abbey just outside the town, the ancient Abbaye de Parc of the Premonstratensian Order or White Canons. It was founded in 1129, and affords to-day an excellent example of a great monastic institution much as it was in the Middle Ages. The outer court is rendered picturesque by the farm buildings which surround it; while the inner contains the dwellings of the canons. The interiors of the main buildings have many handsome rooms in the style of the early part of the eighteenth

Louvain. Tabernacle in Church of St. Pierre.

century, and on the walls are hung some excellent and interesting pictures by Verhaghen, Ernest Quellin, and Michel Coxie.

Louvain as we knew it before the War and Louvain to-day is a very different place. Formerly it had many more ancient houses and quaint

Louvain. Tomb of Matilda of Flanders wife of Henry I.

corners than it now possesses, but those who visit it, will find it still has a general picturesqueness, especially in the northern and western quarters, along the banks of the Dyle.

On the outskirts of Louvain there are many delightful spots and some charming woods. Along the Avenue du Château one comes to a fine manorial estate, once the home of the Count of Arenburg, surrounded by a delightful wood of birches, beeches and other trees. There are winding paths in many directions and in springtime wild flowers, including bluebells, give to the place an added loveliness. There is a story that for some considerable period before the War there were secret comings and goings of German officers and officials and that it was, during the few months immediately preceding the outbreak of War, a hot-bed of spies.

The red brick château, dating from the sixteenth century, was confiscated after the War, the contents were sold,

Louvain. Detail of Tabernacle.

and the fine library of some 50,000 volumes with many rarities dispersed, and at the time of our last visit the building had a forlornly deserted air, notwithstanding it was springtime and all around was beautiful.

In the grounds are many charming vistas of the little river Dyle, which is spanned by several bridges, and there are many tree-shaded walks. In the wood is an old church, set on slightly rising ground and forming a charming picture on a sunny day with patches of light and shade on its white, weather-stained walls.

There are some fragmentary remains of the ancient stronghold of the Counts and Dukes traceable upon the sides and crest of Mont César which rises near the new Benedictine Abbey, close to the Porte de Malines. This eminence is known as Caesar's Castle or the Château de César in perpetuation of the legendary story that it was erected by the Roman Emperor of that name. The Emperor Charles V and his sisters resided at, and were educated in the castle by the famous Adrian Florisz, who afterwards became Pope Adrian VI. There is a fine view of Louvain and its surroundings from the Mont which, for this reason, is well worth climbing.

Louvain. Choir Stalls in St. Gertrude.

Distant view of Liége.

—

CHAPTER III

Liége, its history, picturesqueness and ancient buildings

Liége, which is the capital of the Walloon district of Belgium, the seat of a University and of a Bishop, and formerly the centre of an ecclesiastical principality, is one of the most picturesquely situated and delightful cities in Belgium. It lies chiefly on the high banks of the Meuse, and the river which is broad and swiftly flowing here traverses the whole length of the city, and in doing so forms an island which is connected with each bank by five bridges. The principal part of the city, which is notable in its more modern districts for its broad streets, squares, and delightfully kept gardens and fine public buildings and churches, lies on the left bank while the quarters on the opposite shore, known generally as the Outre Meuse, consist very largely of the factories and dwellings of the artisans.

If one comes to Liége by rail from Antwerp one sees it spread out

Liége. Corner of a market.

beneath one, as the train descends from the high lands above the city to the Station des Guillemins. Before the descent begins one has passed through some of the region of the coal mines which has had so much to do with the industrial prosperity and growth of the city. The latter may be said almost to lie in a basin surrounded by hills, and it was this physical feature that contributed greatly to its weakness strategically in the opening days of the Great War.

The Province of Liége, a land of wooded heights and rushing streams, presents a great contrast to the flat and somewhat uninteresting fields of Flanders and Brabant. It is the country of the Walloons who are noted for their industry, love of freedom and hostility to all who have sought to infringe upon or destroy their privileges and differ so widely in race and speech from their compatriots of northern Belgium. It lies approximately from West to East across Belgium with a somewhat undulating line of demarcation running South of Ypres and North of Liége. In Belgium there are, as is well known, two distinct races the Flemings and the Walloons; and these, in spite of common history, interests and a community of aims, are nevertheless as far apart and distinguishable, in language, appearance, and temperament, as though they actually formed two distinct nations.

The beautiful city of Liége, with its wide quays and fine river, is a very delightful one. The inhabitants in modern times have taken full advantage of the width of the Meuse to beautify their town with ample quays, fine bridges, and many handsome houses

Liége. Place St. Lambert.

and business premises along the riverside. The immediate impression one gains of the city is a pleasant one, for there are handsome public buildings, clean and beautiful boulevards, and a fine river; and the vivacity and cheerfulness of its inhabitants, and the extraordinary beauty of its environment causes it to rank as one of the most picturesque and interesting of European cities.

The history of the town dates from about the seventh century, when Hubert, Bishop of Maestricht, transferred his seat from that town to Liége; and is closely bound up with the empire of Charlemagne during the latter years of the eighth and early years of the ninth centuries. About the end of the tenth century the city, which

Liége. Open air market.

Liége. Park d'Avroy.

previously had been several times raided by the Northmen, was fortified by Bishop Notger, who also destroyed the castles of the adjoining nobles

Liége. A Street Merchant.

in fear that they might prove unwelcome neighbours. Bishop Notger, who was appointed by Otho the Great in 971, may in fact be considered the founder of Liége. It was he who originated the saying " Liége owes Notger to Christ, and everything else she possesses to Notger ". The bishopric by reason of the gifts of Charlemagne and Otho, and their suc-

Liége. View of the Meuse from Citadel.

Liége. Théâtre Royal and Statue of Grétry.

cessors became a very rich one, and by the beginning of the eleventh century the Bishop of Liége had possessed himself of considerable power, his principality including Namur, Dinant, Tongres, Maestricht, Malines, Gembloux and St. Hubert, and so powerful did his successors become that even the proud Counts of Hainault did allegiance to them.

In spite of its industrial side and great metal industries, Liége still keeps much of the beauty and charm of former times. Its situation is both striking and picturesque, for it is built at the confluence of the Ourthe with the Meuse, and the latter river makes another confluence with the Vesdre, thus the town lies in a semi-circle between the hills of St. Walburge, St. Marguerite, and St. Laurent to the west, and Mont Cornillon on the east.

One cannot be in Liége very long before noticing the two great forts which crown the heights above the city and the river. Fort Chartreuse on the right bank, and the ancient Citadel built by Prince Maximilian Henry in 1650 high above the left bank. The views from both of these are well worth the climb, and from the fine tree-shaded promenade near the Citadel one obtains a prospect extending over the beautiful valleys of the Meuse, Ourthe, and Vesdre.

One obtains a very good general idea of the charm of Liége as one comes from the Station des Guillemins along the street of the same name into the wide tree-shaded Boulevard d'Avroy, and through the Park d'Avroy.

One reaches the busy and interesting Place du Théâtre, in the very heart of the city, along the Boulevard de la Sauvenière. The foundation stone of the Théâtre Royal, which has eight rather striking columns of red Belgian marble, was laid by the celebrated Mlle. Mars in 1818. In front of the theatre is the fine bronze statue of Grétry, the Belgian composer, who was born at Liége, by W. Geefs. There is a romantic interest to this statue from the fact that Grétry's heart was at his own request placed in an urn which has been built into the pedestal.

Liége. Courtyard of the Palais de Justice.

West of the Place du Théâtre one finds the Church of St. Jean, which was founded by Bishop Notger in the tenth century, but was rebuilt during the eighteenth. The tower is Romanesque, and goes back to the twelfth century, while the cloisters are even earlier.

Most people will admit to disappointment in regard to the Gothic

Liége. Courtyard of the Palais de Justice.

church of St. Paul, which now serves as the Cathedral. Its exterior, although of architectural interest, it is not imposing. Previous to 1802 the Cathedral was the church of St. Lambert destroyed by the French Revolutionaries. St. Paul's itself dates from the thirteenth century, and occupies the site of a tenth century church. One of the most notable features of the exterior is the portal dating from the thirteenth century, and forming one of the most ancient portions of the building. The interior of the church is very pleasing and elegant. The nave with its round pillars has simplicity and dignity, and is beautified by a good clerestory, and the carved pulpit by Geefs, the idea of which is Truth, is a fine example of nineteenth century sculpture. The best architectural feature of the Cathedral, however, is the choir, which is separated from the nave by an elaborate brass railing, and contains some magnificent stained glass,

Liége. The Inner Court, Palais de Justice.

that in the five windows in the apse dating from the sixteenth century as does also the famous stained glass window in the south transept repre-

senting the Coronation of the Virgin. Much of the modern stained glass, which is beautiful and well worth examining, is by Capronnier. The choir stalls, dating from about 1864, are from designs by Durlet of Antwerp, and represent on the left hand side the Translation of the relics of St. Lambert, and on the right hand side the Resurrection of Believers.

In the south aisle is the modern shrine of St. Lambert, Bishop of Maestricht at the beginning of the eighth century, who was patron saint of Liége. It is made of gilded bronze, with scenes from the

Liége. Staircase of the Provincial Government Building.

life of the Saint in silver panels decorated with enamel and precious stones. In the Treasury are several things worth noting, including the silver gilt reliquary of St. Lambert dating from 1512, a tenth century painting of the Virgin, and a golden group of St. George and Charles the Bold of Burgundy, the work of Gerard Loyet in 1471. This was presented by Charles the Bold in expiation of his destruction of the City in 1468.

From the Cathedral one can easily reach the Palais de Justice, one of the most beautiful buildings in Liége, along the Rue de l'Université and thence through the Place de la République-Française formerly the Place du Théâtre, into the smaller Place du Maréchal-Foch formerly the Place Verte, and finally into the Place St. Lambert. This district is one of the busiest of the shopping quarters of Liége, and mid-day and in the afternoon, whilst walking along the Boulevards and loitering in its pleasant Places, one may gain a very good idea of the Liégeois, their chief characteristics and many types.

The fine Palais de Justice stands on the northern side of the Place St. Lambert. It was once the Episcopal Palace, which was built at the beginning of the sixteenth century by the Prince Bishop Evrard de la Marck, and still retains many features of the original building, and much of its interest notwithstanding the great fire, which in 1735 destroyed its façade and otherwise seriously injured the magnificent old building. There are two charming courts to it, the second of which very greatly resembles the quadrangle of a University in its calm and artistic beauty. Both are surrounded by vaulted arches, which are made up of a curious mixture of various styles of architecture, Gothic, Renaissance, and Moorish. At the beginning of the sixteenth century there lived at Liége one François Borset, a sculptor, and to him must be ascribed most of the grotesque carvings which adorn the capitals of the columns and consist of curious masks, fantastic foliage, figures, etc.

The first court, through which the public pass freely, has been in part restored. The second court, which possesses arcades only on two sides, has been laid out as a garden, and the buildings enclosing it contain, besides the Court rooms, the Archives. The offices of the Provincial Government, which are worth seeing, consist of a series of handsome rooms fitted up to serve on occasion as a Royal residence. The Hall of the Provincial Council is decorated with some fine frescoes of Van Marck, and another hall is hung with old Brussels tapestry by De Leyniers, and several of the adjoining rooms have fine tapestry from Oudenarde.

Perhaps the gems of the building are the Gothic Assize Court, with its handsome chimney piece, and the Throne Room, with its Corinthian columns and fine ceiling, which deserves more than a passing notice. In the buildings surrounding the second court was to be found prior to 1904 the Archaelogical Museum established at the beginning of the seventeenth century. In it there were all kinds of Roman and Frankish antiquities which have been found from time to time in the Province of

Liége, and also the gruesome relic of the body of the Burgomaster Sebastian la Roule, who was murdered by the
Count of Warfuse, on the 17th April 1637.

Opposite the main private entrance to the Palais
de Justice are some charming gardens with fountains,
above which the steep streets rise up the hillside, many
of them having so acute a gradient that they have to
be ascended by means of long flights of steps, such as
the Montagne de Bueren, which lies at the
back of some fine old buildings on the northern
side of the Place St. Lambert and Place du
Marché on the steep flanks of St. Walburga's
Hill, on the summit of which stands the
Citadel.

Following the Rue St. Hubert and
the Rue St. Martin one comes, after
passing St. Croix, to the ancient
church of St. Martin, which
was founded by Bishop
Heraclius in 792. The
present building dates
only from the sixteenth
century. It was in this church
that, during a revolt in 1312,
nearly two hundred nobles of
Liége sought refuge and were
all burned alive.

Not far from the Place St.
Lambert is the Hôtel de Ville,
which was erected in 1714 to
replace the older structure destroyed at the end of the seven-

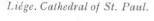

Liége. Cathedral of St. Paul.

teenth century. The architecture of the building is of the type of the Liége
classic of the eighteenth century, and originally the building was very
handsome, but during the period of the Revolution of 1789 it was pillaged
and much damage was done. The Hall, however, remains almost uninjured,
the richly ornamented ceiling of which is supported by eight columns of
black Tuscan marble; and four wooden caryatides, the work of J. Hans,
support a circular tribune with a balustrade of iron work. The staircase is a
handsome and striking one, which ascends from both sides of the Town Hall.

Liége. The Fountain of the steps.

The Place du Marché, one of the four old squares in the middle of the city around which the life of Liége centres, is a wide and restful place, tree-shaded and, in summer, flower-bedecked, having several fine fountains. In the centre of the Place, opposite the Hôtel de Ville stands the graceful Fontaine du Perron, or Fontaine des Trois-Grâces, with its arcading and lofty column, the work of Delcour in 1696. The Liégeois are immensely proud of this fountain, which has, indeed, become historic, and is one of the artistic treasures which everyone is expected to see. Near the Western end of the Cathedral of St. Paul stands another fountain of Delcour surmounted by a figure

of the Virgin. These are two of the many works of art by this master with which he beautified the city.

. Standing just out of the market place is the Hôtel d'Ansenborg, which was formerly the property of the Counts d'Ansenborg, in the Rue Féronstrée running out of the market place. It was purchased by the city in 1903 and is now used as a Museum of Decorative Art. It is remarkable for its beautifully carved ceiling and staircases. One of the most

Liége. The Delcour Fountain.

interesting rooms in the building is the kitchen which is entirely lined with Delft tiles, the big fire place is also tiled, and the chimney piece is supported by pilasters. Another room, which never fails to please, is the charming small hall situated on the first floor, which

Liége. Reliquary of St. Lambert (Detail).

has a beautiful painted ceiling, a fine chimney piece, and fire-place over which is a portrait of the founder Michel Willems. The whole museum is one of the most delightful of its kind in Belgium, and

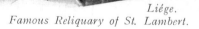

Liége.
Famous Reliquary of St. Lambert.

contains many treasures of art, and some interesting drawings and engravings by early Liége masters including examples of Lambert Lom-

Liége. Pulpit Church of St. Jacques.

bard 1505-1566 down to Leonard de France 1735-1805 and later masters.

Beyond the Salon Rouge is the staircase, which is remarkable for its fine ironwork balustrading and proportions. The ceiling on the top floor is an admirable example of stucco work, consisting of birds, figures, and geometrical designs. Many of the sitting rooms contain fine examples of furniture in the style of Louis XIV and Louis XV, beautiful pieces of Brussels tapestry, and handsomely carved wooden shutters. The large hall to the left of the entrance, which was ori-

Liége. Nave of the Cathedral.

ginally the music room, is a magnificent apartment with a handsome mantelpiece of white marble, a fine chimney piece, and a beautifully designed stucco ceiling; while the high windows running right up to the frieze and the narrow mirrors between them, and fine Brussels tapestry hangings, representing hunting scenes from David Teniers, pictures, which came from the ancient Château de Saive, and furniture in the

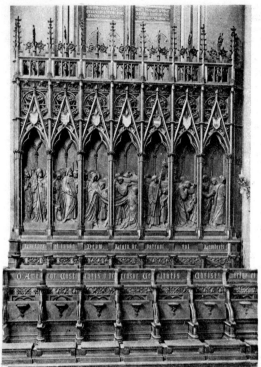

Liége. Cathedral Stalls.

Louis XV style complete a delightful room conveying a clear impression of the artistic achievements and luxury of that age.

At the eastern end of the wide Quai de Maestricht, not far from the Pont St. Leonard, stands the Museum of Arms so closely connected with one of the chief industries for which the town has for centuries been famous. The Mortars at the entrance were cast in the early days of the nineteenth century at the Liége arms fac-

tory, and there is much of curious interest in the Museum itself for students of by-gone weapons.

One should certainly cross the river to visit the Church of St. Jacques, one of the most interesting ecclesiastical buildings in Liége, which, founded in the eleventh century with a twelfth century western façade, forms a relic of the original building. Practically the whole of the remainder of the church is very Late Gothic of the sixteenth century, and of the florid architecture of that period it is a very perfect example, and at the same time far more pleasing in execution than the majority of churches of the type.

The interior of the church forms a wonderful

Liége. Bust of St. Lambert.

Liége. Church of St. Jacques. The organ loft.

example of elaborate decoration, and creates amazement at the infinite labour and skill which must have gone to the production of the ornate ceiling of the nave, and the elaborate decorated arches of the transepts. The fine choir derives not a little of its effectiveness and beauty from the lighting afforded by its seven magnificent sixteenth century windows.

Unfortunately of late years the stone carving has been considerably spoiled by paint, but the many excellent statues by Delcour remain unspoiled, and the very elaborate decorations are saved from giving an impression of confusion by the fine proportions of the choir. The transepts and nave are practically the same in design, and it must be confessed are somewhat bewildering in the ornateness of the decorations of arches and galleries, and their somewhat bizarre colour schemes. The organ, built by André Séverin of Maestricht in 1673, deserves special note. Séverin in buried in the cloisters, and the epitaph which adorns his tomb runs as follows; — " André Séverin unequalled in his Art has made for us in this organ one of his marvels. Born at Maestricht, he died, and rests full of honours in these cloisters. "

No one can pass along the river front at Liége without being struck by a remarkable building of limestone and brick, with a lofty roof and tower and curious sculptures, standing beneath the Citadel hill. It is the Curtius Museum built by one Jean Curtius in 1600, afterwards used as the Mont de Piété, or Municipal Pawnshop, but since 1904 the home of the Archaeological Museum, formerly housed in the Palais de Justice. The Museum contains a valuable collection of pre-historic Gallo-Roman and Frankish antiquities, found chiefly in the Province of Liége and some especially valuable of the era of Charlemagne. Among the principal objects is a bronze ewer and basin of the Roman period, a ticket of discharge of one of the Emperor Trajan's legionaries about 98 A. D., a stamp of a Roman physician, and a fine coloured relief of the Madonna dating from the eleventh century. The staircase of the house has ornamental wrought iron balustrading of great artistic merit, dating from the eighteenth century. It is so constructed that the landing looks as though it were a bridge. The ceiling with its narrow beams and vaulting is very original, and dates from the beginning of the seventeenth century, and over one of the doorways on the landing is a curious group of four sculptured figures.

One of the most interesting survivals in the house is the apartment on the first floor with its beautiful decorated chimneypiece dating from the sixteenth century, and the original casement window;

Liége. Quai de Maestricht and Curtius Museum.

and on the mantelpiece are to be noticed some delightful figurines.

Liége, of course, is a city of churches, and one may mention amongst others worth seeing that of St. Denis in the Rue de Cathédrale, where there is a fine sixteenth century altar piece of wood carving representing scenes of the Saviour's Passion, and events in the life of St. Denis. Another is the twelfth century church of St. Barthélemy, with its two Romanesque towers. In this is a large bronze font which rests on the backs of ten brass oxen, and is embellished with scriptural scenes in relief. This wonderful font was cast in 1112 by Renier de Huy for the Abbey of Orval. It is perhaps one of the most celebrated examples of the metal workers of Dinant.

The only other important building to notice in Liége is the University, which one reaches from the Place du Théâtre along the Rue de l'Université. This seat of learning which stands facing the Place Cockerill on the Quai de l'Université, but a little distance from the bank of the Meuse, has experienced strange vicissitudes during the time which has elapsed since its foundation by the Jesuits in the last days of the Prince Bishops of Liége. It was a Central School during the Revolutionary period, and a Lycée or Public School under the Empire, and was made a University in 1817 by the Dutch Government for the Walloon District, who gathered together Professors from France and Germany to supervise its studies. The library contains about 320,000 volumes, and some

Liége. Along the Quays.

1400 MSS. Attached at various times to this seat of learning have been many eminent Professors including St. Beuve, Emile de Laveleye, and Catalan.

But to those who have been accustomed to the beautiful buildings of Oxford and Cambridge, and those of some of the older English Public Schools, Liége University will strike a note rather of utility than of beauty and antiquity.

On one side of the Quai de l'Université the river is spanned by the Pont de la Boverie, and on the other the " Passerelle " or Footbridge. From either of these, one obtains delightful views of the river either up or down stream. The view up stream is perhaps the prettier because of the beautiful curve, and the trees which border the river side, especially those of the Jardin d'Acclimatation. Several other bridges span the river in either direction, and as is their wont help to beautify it. The fine Pont des Arches, built some 70 years ago, replaced a former

Seraing. Cockerill Works.

structure which since the 17th century had been the only means of communication with the opposite bank.

Above Liége towers the Citadel, 520 feet above sea level, built by

Unloading a barge on the Meuse.

the Prince Bishop Maximilien after the siege of Liége in 1649, when the city was captured by the Elector of Cologne. The view from the roadway and the terraced path above the city is a very extensive and beautiful one, embracing as it does not only Liége itself and its outlying quarters, but the Valleys of the Meuse, the Ourthe and the Vesdre. The prospect is bounded towards the south by the mountains of the

Ardennes, and towards the north it reaches to the Petersberg near Maestricht, with the broad plains of Limburg beyond.

On the opposite bank of the Meuse one sees the abandoned fort known as La Chartreuse, which commands a very charming prospect quite different in character. The best point of view is the ancient garden of the Hospice de la Chartreuse, an institution for old men, which lies half way up the hill along the road of the Montagne de la Chartreuse. One can reach the higher ground of Robermont by electric tram where there is a fine cemetery near which the Prince of Coburg was defeated by the French under Marshal Jourdan on September 16th 1794.

Liége. Lintel of door from Huy in Curtius Museum.

Ardennes. Countryside near Chaudfontaine.

CHAPTER IV

—

Some Meuse Valleys and their Castles — Spa and its springs and the Hautes Fagnes

Two miles from Liége, at Chênée, the Ourthe is joined by its tributary the Vesdre before flowing into the Meuse. Formerly it was a most beautifully pellucid stream, but now-a-days it is contaminated by the refuse of the factories at Verviers, and the mines near Liége. Rising in Rhenish Prussia its tortuous course extends for some fifty miles, of which about thirty are in Belgium. A little way up the Vesdre and one comes to Vaux-sous-Chévremont, at the foot of a hill which is now crowned by a seventeenth century oratory, formerly much resorted to by pilgrims, but in early days the site was that of the impregnable fortress of Chévremont, which was destroyed by Bishop Notger.

Still further on in this delightfully picturesque district one reaches

Chaudfontaine. On the Vesdre.

Chaudfontaine, with its charming half-circle of cultivated land shut in by wooded hills, its tiny church, and houses clustering on the river bank, and with a graceful suspension bridge spanning the stream, and leading to the little Kursaal which in summer is the centre of the holiday life of the place. The warm springs, to which the little town owes its fame, were discovered as long ago as the thirteenth century. Then by some mischance their existence was forgotten until the seventeenth century, when Simon Sauveur obtained permission to erect a small building with baths round one of the springs.

Wonderful cures were effected, and an attempt was made to obtain a definite concession of the land from the Bishop of Liége. Finally in 1713 the concession of the spring was granted to Sauveur's heirs in return for the curious rent of 200 capons. The Hôtel des Bains was built, and a suitable road constructed from Liége to Chaudfontaine. It is still as ever a great resort on Sundays of the Liégeois, who then make their way thither in crowds mostly by motor car, but even to-day also in horse vehicles of almost every kind. In the near vicinity are several fine Châteaux, such as in medieval times were thickly strewn all over the Ardennes.

Lion of Belgium on the Gileppe Barrage.

Pepinster for most people is only a small town where there is a railway junction between Liége and Spa, but it really is a pretty little place where the beautiful valleys of the Vesdre and Hoegne join. Up the charming valley of the latter lies Juslenville with its Château once the home of Pauline Borghese. Some years ago an important Gallo-Roman burial place was discovered among the hills near Juslenville, in which many ornaments and implements of antiquarian value have from time to time been discovered. High above the little town stands the church amid the trees; and still further up the valley is the ancient eleventh century town of Theux, a delightful spot, and a place of quaint aspect which, notwithstanding its ironworks and cloth factories, has managed to preserve much of its old-world and picturesque appearance. Its ancient church has a

somewhat remarkable tower, the ceiling of which is of wood, with the panels painted with the heads of saints. Among other things worth noting in this building are two Holy Water vessels of the fourteenth century, six fifteenth century frescoes, and a Romanesque font. Close to the town, at the place where the Wayai falls into the Hoegne, is a rocky eminence on which are the ruins of the ancient castle of Franchimont. The Prince Bishops of Liége seized the property in 1048, and converted it into a residence for their Lieut-Governors. The

The Church at Theux.

View of the Barrage of Gileppe.

last proprietor is said to have been a robber knight, from whom the Bishops seized the castle, and who possessing vast treasures buried them in the vaults, where they remain hidden to this day. Sir Walter Scott refers to this tradition in his lines on the Towers of Franchimont :

> " Which, like an eagle's nest in air
> Hangs o'er the stream and hamlet fair,
> Deep in their vaults, the peasants say,
> A mighty treasure buried lay,
> Amass'd through rapine and through wrong
> By the last Lord of Franchimont. "

Below the Château lies the hamlet of Marché de Theux, which takes its name from the fairs which in ancient times were held there. The Château appears to have been in a fair state of repair until the French Revolution, when it was attacked by the people, sacked and burned. Over the doorway of the entrance are still to be seen three coats of arms, those of Franchimont, Bavaria, from Bishop Ernest of Bavaria who restored the castle in 1581, and of Aspremont Lynden. The walls of the castle are of considerable extent and of great thickness, and the Keep, with its round isolated tower on the south, contains the remains of a circular staircase,

Château de Franchimont and view of Theux.

with towers united by a " curtain ". Hereabouts the walls have a thickness of nearly 25 feet, so that one can well imagine the strength of the
castle in the stormy days when it was a fortress often assailed.

It is Jean d'Ardenne, the writer who has so closely studied the history,
topography, and myths of the Ardennes who deals at some length with
the legend of the Green Goat of Franchimont which is supposed to haunt
the ruins of the Castle and guard
the treasure hidden in its vaults
by the robber knight.

It is round about here that
one meets, along the tortuous and
narrow roads, the picturesquely
attired women of the
Ardennes. They belong to
a race that has few equals
in Europe, for they pos-
sess, added to the thrift
of their neighbours the
French, the hardihood

Château de Franchimont.

and courage which seems to distinguish mountain peoples, and have not a little kinship with the women of Switzerland. Even to-day in the more remote districts, picturesque bullock carts add a note of quaintness to

A peep at Spa.

the traffic of the highways. Although distinctive costume is not quite so prevalent in the Ardennes as some years ago, one still meets with women knitting as they go along the high road, wearing high crowned straw hats tied under the chin, and satin or fabric aprons of gay colours.

Dropped down in this charming region, whose little towns and scattered villages seem so remote from the highest forms of modern civilisation, and, let it be said, modern materialism, we come upon the delightful and picturesque town of Spa, one of the most famous watering places of Europe. It is very modern, although here and there fragments of the old time Spa are left for the curious to discover. Distant only some twenty miles from Liége it is little to be wondered at that so delightfully situated a spot should have long ago become one of the most popular holiday resorts not only with the Liégeois, but with well-to-do Belgians from all parts of the kingdom. Spa is one of the most interesting places in the Province of Liége not only on account of the delightful scenery of its valley, which is watered by clear flowing streams originating in the high plateaux which lie above it to the east and south, but also from the many associations of past days, when it was thronged by the illustrious and celebrated of former generations.

It is difficult, indeed, on arriving in Spa to conceive how it is that this gem of a pleasure resort set in a valley and between heights of great beauty can have entirely escaped, as it has, the destroying influence of industrial progress. Here are all the amenities of a fashionable resort wedded to much picturesqueness of architecture, and surrounded by great natural beauty, while less than twenty miles away are humming factories, with chimneys belching forth thick volumes of smoke, chemical works, vast pyramids of black slag, and all the ugliness of a coal mining district.

Spa. The Parish Church.

In spite of the coldness of the climate, for Spa is from 800 to nearly 1100 feet above sea level, and rather frequent changes of temperature, the town is considered one of the healthiest resorts in Europe. It has a short season because winter releases its hold upon Spa with reluctance, and summer does not linger in the valley. But at the height of the season it is, indeed, a delightful place thronged with well-dressed people bent upon enjoyment; the invalids seem to the average visitor at such times almost negligible, and there is plenty of amusement to be had; — tennis, golf, horseracing, dancing, swimming, motoring to many delightful spots, whilst the Casino provides unrivalled music, and a constant round of gaiety. And then there is the brilliant sunshine of a comparatively high plateau, and the wealth and beauty of the flowers, in the gardens, in the grounds of the Casino, in beds along the boulevards under the trees, and in the shops. In June and July a very definite impression that Spa is a town of floral loveliness is left upon the mind of the visitor.

Its reputation, due to the presence of its famous Springs, dates from the sixteenth century, when in the reign of Charles V it became a rival to Baden Baden. Towards the end of the eighteenth century, however, the town became known rather as a centre of social life for the aristocracy of Europe than as a health resort pure and simple. Indeed, one of its frequenters Joseph II designated it the Café de l'Europe. Formerly a tiny Ardennes town, frequented not for its social attractions but for its springs, it underwent a startling development; hotels to accommodate the famous people who came to it, handsome buildings to afford facilities for amusement, and fine villas sprang up side by side with the unpretentious dwellings of the original inhabitants, and in course of time replaced most of these. Good roads, and promenades were laid out and the transformation of Spa was complete. Gambling became fashionable, and considerable notoriety was earned by the little town in this respect. Then came the outbreak of the French Revolution, and on the approach of the Republican armies those members of the nobility who had lingered in the town took flight to the banks of the Rhine, and Spa suffered an eclipse.

Both the Revolution of 1830 and the suppression of gambling in 1872 proved disastrous to the town which, however, gradually recovered, and to-day is again one of the most fashionable and delightful health resorts in Europe. Its present vogue is largely owing to its natural beauty, the enduring reputation of its waters, and the great efforts that have been made by its municipal authorities to keep abreast of the times in the sports, pastimes, and amusements which are provided for visitors.

Spa is a very different place to-day from what it was in the sixteenth century when the famous Venetian physician of Henry VIII, Agostino by name, visited it, or when Margaret of Valois came in 1577, and wrote of it in her diary as a little village of three or four wretched houses ! That Spa, notwithstanding its modernness, is really a historic place is vouched for by the fact that the names of the Merrie Monarch, Cosimo de Medici, Peter the Great, Queen Christina of Denmark, Gustavus the Third of

Spa. The Kursaal.

Sweden, the Emperor Joseph II, Louis Philippe of Orléans, the first
Emperor of United Germany, the Duke of Wellington, and the composer
Meyerbeer figure on its roll of visitors. All of them are depicted in a
painting in the Hall of the Pouhon, one of the rooms of the fine building
which covers the most fashionable of the various Springs of Spa.

The chief commercial asset of Spa is its numerous mineral springs,
of which the Sauvenière is considered to be the oldest. Some authorities,
indeed, assert that it is to this spring
Pliny makes allusion in speaking of a
celebrated spring in the Country of
Tongres. The ancient Roman writer
wrote " Tungri, a State in Gaul,
has a remarkable spring, with
many bubbles, tasting of iron. "
The springs at Tongres are still
in action, but rather inferior in
quality, and the remains of a
Roman road near the Sauvenière

Spa. A goat carriage.

doubtless gave rise to the idea that Pliny may have referred to the Spring at Spa.

Near the Promenade des Anglais is the pretty, artificial lake of Warfaz, rather more than a third of a mile in length, on which much boating takes place in the season. Another delightful Promenade is that named after Meyerbeer, who was a frequent visitor to Spa.

Spa. The Windmill on the Promenade de Sept-Heures.

The chief buildings are the Casino, and the fine modern church with twin towers which form a very striking feature of the landscape when the town is viewed from the heights. The Casino or Kursaal is a magnificent building, which was completed in 1908, and almost entirely burnt down in the following year, but was speedily rebuilt. The huge concert hall has seating accommodation for several thousand people, and contains in addition a ballroom, theatre, reading rooms, and café restaurant, with a delightful terrace, which in the season is crowded with fashionable folk taking afternoon tea.

There are several delightful parks and gardens, and among the most pleasant is the Promenade de Sept-Heures, with its beautiful avenue of elms, placed at the foot of the

Spa.
Château de Neubois.
The Ex-Kaisers'
Headquarters.

Montagne d'Annette et Lubin which was laid out in 1750 by the Archbishop of Augsburg. From the Montagne d'Annette et Lubin or Spalou-

Spa. Pavilion of the Promenade de Sept-Heures.

mont, which dominates Spa to the north, one obtains some of the finest views of the town, and surrounding country. The "Montagne" is ascended by many delightful paths through its wooded heights, in most places the climb is made fairly easily by the care with which the gradients have been arranged. The Artists' Walk, as it is called, is one of the best known in the woods, and in late spring or early autumn its charm is

Spa.
The Ex-Kaiser's "Dug-out".

Spa. The Road to Malmédy.

not easily overrated. It descends the course of a little stream presenting in succession scenes of woodland beauty not easily surpassed in any equally frequented spot. It must inevitably remind the English visitor not a little of the scenery of Watersmeet in the Valley of the Lyn at Lynmouth in North Devon.

Although Spa is so essentially a pleasure and health resort with its chief interests centred in the accommodation, and entertainment of its visitors, it yet possesses one staple industry - the manufacture of painted and varnished articles of wood known locally as " Bois de Spa ". This industry and art began in the

Inlaid woodwork of Spa.

View in the Hautes-Fagnes.

eighteenth century, and has varied very considerably from time to time according to the demands of customers, the changes of fashion, and the inventiveness and spirit of the artist. Many of the older specimens made in the earlier periods of the development of this local art are very beautiful, much sought after, and were the work of craftsmen of great skill and high reputation.

Visitors to Spa since the Great War, have sought at least to get a glimpse of the Château de Neubois, on the outskirts of the town on the main road to Sart, from the fact that it was

A wayside Inn in the Ardennes.

Château de Rémouchamps in the Valley of the Amblève.

here that the Kaiser had his headquarters during the War. Beneath the lawn, surrounding this delightful country house, which is rather English in style of architecture, were constructed steel and concrete rooms to which the Emperor and his family retreated when any Allied aeroplanes made their appearance.

The great Barrage de la Gileppe north of Jalhay, formed as a resevoir for the supply of water to Verviers and other towns through an aqueduct five and a half miles in length, never fails to interest the visitor. Prominent on the Barrage is an enormous representation of the Lion of Belgium upon a lofty pedestal weighing many tons.

Stavelot some fifteen miles south-east of Spa is a rather charming little town on the banks of the Amblève. It is chiefly noted for its tanneries, but most people will be more interested in its churches, and the delightful and ancient Hospice. The founder of the Abbey is said to have been St. Remacle, Bishop of Maestricht who died in A. D. 666. The Abbey church was built in the 11th century, and of this a tower and the porch still stand. The other buildings, which include the Abbot's Palace, rebuilt in the eighteenth century, are now the Hospice Ferdinand Nicoli. Among the treasures of the Parish Church is the Châsse de St. Remacle, a beau-

Cascade de Coo.

Country Scene between Stavelot and Malmédy.

tifully enamelled and jewelled reliquary of the thirteenth century, and also that of St. Popol who was the builder of the Abbey Church. The latter was almost entirely destroyed at the Revolution. One strange thing which is sure to strike the visitor to Stavelot, is the fact that the gardens of the townsfolk instead of being attached to the houses are placed apart on the outskirts, very much as are the allotments in many English towns.

Those who would know something of the southern Ardennes should certainly make their way down the beautiful Valleys of the Amblève and the Ourthe. They will come to Trois-Ponts, where there is the well known Cascade de Coo, a pretty, though artificial cataract, which has served to make the little town famous, and much visited in the summer months. It owes its origin to Jacques Hubin, Abbot of Stavelot, at the end of the eighteenth century. A three mile curve of the Amblève comes back to within a few yards of the starting point, and the monks of the Abbey joined the two waters by cutting through the intervening piece of rock.

From Coo one goes on down the picturesque valley, the road mostly following the river course fairly closely, until one comes to the famous grotto of Remouchamps situated on the right bank of the Amblève,

which here becomes navigable. Though in no way comparing either in regard to size or interest with the famous grottos of Han and Rochefort, Remouchamps is quite well worth visiting, as are also the ruins of the Château of Amblève, which stands on a pre-cipitous rock 400 feet high, and was once the residence of the Quatre Fils d'Aymon, and in later times of William de la Marck. The river Amblève here is particularly de-lightful, and crystal clear.

One goes on pleasantly to Esneux on the Ourthe which forms a very good centre from which to explore the val-ley, and vicinity of that river. Esneux is a delightful little place situated on a peninsula formed by a wide bend of the river. The surrounding hills are sharply silhouetted against the sky, and the water flows lazily beneath the arches of the bridge, at the end of which

Reliquary of St. Remacle at Stavelot.

stands a quaint little hotel, in summertime com-pletely covered with climbing roses. Above the town lies the Plateau of Hamay, and the height of Beaumont, and from these vantage points the traveller enjoys magnificent views of the town and the Valley of the Ourthe.

But a little way further down this delightful valley which, indeed, is so full of charming spots one is reluc-tantly compelled to pass over without description, one comes to Tilff. It is a charmingly situated little town on the banks of the river which seen from the heights on either hand presents a very picturesque appearance,

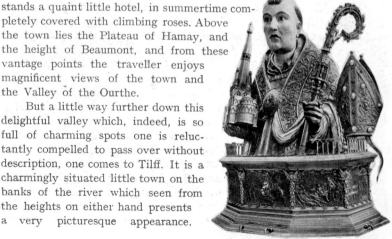

Reliquary of St. Popol at Stavelot.

A tributary of the Amblève.

View of Malmédy.

Near by is the great limestone cavern known as the Grotto of Tilff, discovered nearly a century ago by quarrymen, and full of curious stalactites. In the church near the bridge is a reliquary said to contain a piece of the true Cross, and not far from the church stands the Château of Sauvage with its delightful gardens and lawns.

A few miles takes the traveller to the entrance of the valley, where stands the Château of Kimkempois not far from the point where the Ourthe joins the Vesdre in wide convolutions ere flowing into the Meuse. Away to the south-east of Liége, and extending from the Amblève as far as the German frontier and beyond, lies the wide Plateau known as the Hautes Fagnes, and in the district is included Spa and the Baraque Michel, which is the highest point in Belgium, and marks the greatest altitude between the basins of the Rhine, Meuse, and Moselle. The barren soil of the heather-clad Fagnes provides a striking contrast to that of the beautiful and cultivated valleys, which, as is the case with that of Spa lie close beside these desolate wastes. Here and there the grim monotony of the Plateau is broken by stretches of marshy ground and dark bogland, or by clumps of stunted firs, and stray beeches and dwarfed oaks, which have somehow or other gained a foot-hold in the uncongenial soil. This lonely moorland district inevitably reminds one of some portions of Scotland. On the borders of the Fagnes lie scattered a few hamlets and farms, the low walls and thatched roofs of which are often over-topped by the thick hedges of hornbeam which have been planted to give them shelter. The winds of this desolate-looking and inclement Plateau are often very tempestuous, and the winter is extremely severe, snow sometimes lying for weeks together, so that the inhabitants are isolated from each other. In summertime the heatherland and stunted woods become dry as tinder, and great fires often take place burning miles and miles of heather, and at the beginning of the eighteenth century a conflagration of this kind burnt on for weeks until it was at length put out by the autumnal rains.

Archaeologists have discovered traces of Roman roads passing through the desolate Fagnes, and there are now-a-days several quite good highways crossing it in various directions. The Baraque Michel, 2215 feet, can be reached on foot from Spa by way of Sart or from Hockai on the Luxembourg line, from which it is only about four miles distant. One traverses along the road to the Baraque Michel flat marshy land close to the German frontier, but when one has attained the summit there is a magnificent prospect spread out before one. To the south is the lovely

Malmédy. View on the Wache on the road to Spa.

Valley of the Salm, and on the north the Valley of the Meuse, and Maestricht and the district round Aix-la-Chapelle. Westward lies the Province of Liége as far as Brabant.

On Baraque Michel no fewer than seven streams have their source; the Roer, the Helle, the Sauer, the Gileppe, the Hoegne, the Eau Rouge, and the Wache. Years ago, indeed, this was a desolate place and the name Baraque or Hut recalls a story of a certain tailor, Michel Schmidt of Jalhay, who in the winter of 1808 was overtaken by darkness on the mountain, and planted his stick in the snow, and vowed to heaven that if the lived through the night and escaped he would henceforth devote his life to rescuing travellers who found themselves in a like position of danger. He was true to his word, and built a hut on the summit of the hill; and his son, and afterwards his grandson, duly carried out the duties of custodian of the hut which was built in 1826. Adjoining this is the Chapelle Fishbach, built in 1830 by an inhabitant of Stavelot to commemorate his rescue, after he had lost his way on the moor during a hunting expedition.

Not far from the Baraque stand the ruins of Peter's Huis, formerly an old Hospice for Travellers. The owners of the building, however, were, so the story goes, in the habit of robbing and murdering unfortunate wayfarers, and for these crimes they were at last hanged in chains and the building destroyed.

The Ourthe at Esneux.

The Meuse at Namèche.

CHAPTER V

—

The Meuse from Liége to Namur — The Ardennes
Arlon — Chiny — Bouillon — Laroche

Notwithstanding the fact that there are several industrial towns on the banks of the Meuse from Liége up to Namur there is much delightful scenery, some of it extremely fine, where the river runs through what is practically a rocky and in most places a tree-clad gorge with many tiny valleys running inland from both sides of the river with fern-clad banks and crevices, and sparkling streams, some of the latter turning picturesque water mills.

At Huy the river flows in a rather restricted valley between high and verdure-clad cliffs, and exhibits some of the most typical scenery and beauty of its course. Even in Huy itself, and in the villages on either hand of it, mostly placed almost at the water's edge, the factories which have sprung up appear powerless greatly to impair the natural beauty of the countryside. Huy is on the right bank of the Meuse, and at the confluence with its tributaries the Hoyoux and Mehaigne. Few towns of a similar character in Belgium surpass Huy in the natural beauty of its situation. Close to it comes a sharp bend in the river, and lofty tree-clad hills and vineyards rise on either hand forming a charming prospect which never fails to delight.

Seen from the left bank of the river, from or not far from the old seven-arched stone bridge, the town presents a very picturesque appearance most of it being built along the waterside with the fine twin-towered church of Notre Dame set a little back, and the cliffs behind the town crowned by the huge Citadel which was built by the Dutch in the first quarter of the nineteenth century, and added to in 1892. This rises from the river in terraces, and some of the works are actually constructed in the rock itself. It occupies the site of an ancient Castle the origin of which is lost in the mists of time. At the end of the tenth century this became the property of the Prince Bishop of Liége, who frequently came and resided in it, particularly when there was trouble with the inhabitants

Huy. The little Square.

Huy. The Bridge and Citadel.

of his Cathedral city. In common with many other castles of the Meuse Valley that of Huy sustained constant sieges right from the beginning of the eleventh century down to the time of its destruction by the Dutch at the beginning of the eighteenth. Under the shadow of the Citadel and at its foot stands the church of Notre Dame, one of the finest Gothic churches in Belgium. Perhaps the feature that strikes one first on viewing it is its lack of width. But built as it is between the Castle and the Meuse the architect was necessarily compelled to adapt himself to the exigencies of the site chosen. The chief front has no access, entrance being by two doors at either side. The church was begun in 1311, but suffered very serious damage by fire, and was largely rebuilt in the sixteenth century. No one should miss noticing the beautiful western portal with an elaborate rose window, and some good sculpture. The famous Bethlehem portal with its remarkable sculptures stands detached from the remainder of the building at its eastern end. Formerly the entrance to cloisters, it was built as early as the thirteenth century.

The interior, which is very impressive and beautiful, is mainly of black limestone which, although it tends to an unusually sombre appearance, undoubtedly strengthens the impression of dignity. The nave,

Huy. The Fountain.

however, is magnificently lighted by great windows, and the Arabesque paintings of the roof, even if they seem somewhat out of character with the simplicity of the general design, have the effect of adding lightness to the building.

The nave is triple with chapels at the side, and it will be noted that the perfect harmony has been somewhat injured by the restorations which followed the fire of 1499. The side chapels are very ornamental, and the Gothic altar screen and carved pulpit are both worthy of attention. The treasury of the church possesses several ancient chests described as those of the Virgin, St. Mark, St. Mangold, and St. Domitian which are excellent examples of the beautiful work of medieval craftsmen. The chest of the Virgin dates from the beginning of the thirteenth century and is very richly decorated with enamels and reliefs, and those of St. Mangold and St. Domitian are at least a century older.

One of the most picturesque cosrner of the town is a little square, at the point where the Pont des Chaines crosses the river, tree-shadowed and surrounded by some of the older houses, and affording a picturesque peep of the towers and a portion of the church of Notre Dame. Here are set up market stalls, and there is always a gay little flower market here during the summer months.

A Candlestick at Huy.

Huy. View of Cathedral.

Huy. Interior of Cathedral.

At the end of the Meuse Promenade to the north of the town formerly stood the Abbey of Neufmoustier founded by Peter the Hermit, the preacher of the Crusade in 1100, who was buried in 1115 in the crypt of the church. In 1633 his remains were exhumed, and placed in a shrine or châsse. At the suppression of the Religious Houses the church was destroyed, as were most of the Abbey buildings. To-day a statue of Peter the Hermit stands on the spot where he was formerly buried. Neufmoustier was one of seventeen religious houses which Huy, with a population of not more than 5.000, possessed in the Middle Ages.

Quite near Huy are many places of interest and some delightful scenery. One of the most famous of the châteaux in the district is that of Modave built picturesquely on a rock near the junction of the Hoyoux and the Bonne. The origin of the château goes back to the Roman occupation, and the construction of a fortress dates from early feudal times. In the fourteenth century the château was made more habitable, but it was not until the seventeenth century that it was reconstructed, more or less in the form in which we find it to-day, by Count Jean Gaspard de Marchin, one of whose descendants Ferdinand, a Marshal of France, sold it.

The most interesting part of the castle is the wonderful entrance hall, the ceiling being very curious with the genealogy of the family de Marchin worked out in coloured reliefs until the fourth degree, while the frieze is composed of coats of arms of members of the family.

One of the most interesting rooms is the cabinet called the Boudoir of the Duke, ornamented with painted panels by the Liége artists Coelens and Morel, the ceiling and frieze are very handsome, and the former is supported by carved caryatides between the panelling. From this room one gains a delight-ful view of the beautiful park, and the wind-ings of the Hoyoux flowing in the hol-low of the gorge.

Andenne which lies almost mid-way between Huy and Namur on the right bank of the Meuse is a small but pic-turesquely situated town the chief in-dustries of which are paper making, faience, and pot-tery. It is chiefly interesting as providing a good example of a typi-cal Belgian manu-facturing town which has grown up from the Middle Ages onwards around an impor-tant religious community. The

Huy. The Bethlehem Portal.

Convent is said to have been founded by St. Begge, who was the daughter of Pepin of Landen, and the Order was probably identical with, or at any rate closely approximated that of the Béguines. The church still remaining is an interesting building of considerable size containing a fine Renaissance reliquary of St. Begge, and also a famous miracle-working tablet of the saint, the healing virtues of which were in the Middle Ages highly esteemed not only by the people of the district round about, but also by those in other parts of the Meuse Valley.

From Andenne the river runs in broad curves to Selignaux past Sclaigneaux where there are curiously jagged red cliffs, and a quaint Romanesque church, to Namèche in the midst of fruit trees and pleasant fields, and Samson, a tiny village nestling at the foot of picturesque cliffs of white limestone. And so to Marché-les-Dames with its great iron works, and the ruins of the fine Château of the Prince of Arenburg, placed amongst the trees on the rocky slopes above the river, standing on the site of a famous Abbey built in the first year of the twelfth century by over a thousand women of noble birth, widows of the Crusaders who had fallen in the Holy Land, serving under Godfrey de Bouillon.

The most important part of the ancient Forest of Ardennes, the

Château of Marché-les-Dames.

The Meuse at Marché-les-Dames.

greatest and most famous one in Gaul, lies in Luxembourg, which is the largest and least populous of the nine Provinces of Belgium. At the time of Julius Caesar the Forest of Ardennes extended from the borders of the Rhine and the boundaries of the Treviri as far as the limits of the Nervii.

In the Belgian Ardennes there are still some of the finest woods in Europe, which have come down through the ages to us very little altered in character from what they were in the days of Caesar. Very delightful portions of the great forest are the woods around Laroche, those of St. Hubert, of Chiny on the Semois, and of Amerois and Herbeumont.

The Ardennes district, which has been called " Switzerland in minia-ture, " is the most picturesque portion of Belgium, and comprises moun-tains, table lands and valleys abounding with views sometimes very rugged and wild, at others rural, and always picturesque. It forms one of the favourite holiday grounds of the Belgian people, and much of the region is almost unknown to the tourists and holiday makers of other countries, though year by year more English people are discovering its beauties and charm. In a rough and on the whole rugged land one finds magnificent stretches of pre-historic forest with thick vegetation, and

Landscape in the Ardennes.

here and there expanses of green fields hemmed in by charming hills, and watered by clear rivulets, flowing peacefully or noisily as the case may be through pleasant valleys and rocky gorges. And as a contrast to this scenery there are the wild heath-clad uplands where spring into being streams destined to become turbulent torrents hemmed in along their course by bare and rugged rocks.

The Ardennes area is well watered by the Ourthe, the Semois, the Amblève, the Sure, the Lomme, the Salm, and many other streams. The general elevation of the country is about 500 feet above sea level, but the hills and wild plateaux which form prominent characteristics of the scenery range from 1200 to 1500 feet. The Ardennes offers both varied and great attractions to the holiday maker and to the artist, for one has in it richly wooded heights and dells; rugged rocks, crowned by crumbling ruins of châteaux and medieval fortresses; and fertile valleys occupied by small but flourishing villages, and by picturesque hamlets whose mere handful of inhabitants seem to dwell there entirely untroubled by the doings and convulsions political and otherwise of the bustling outside world.

One of the most picturesquely situated of the larger towns of the

Ardennes is Arlon, the capital of the Belgian Province of Luxembourg. A very ancient place, it is situated on a high well-wooded tableland and commands extensive views, some of the finest of which are obtained from the terrace of the church of St. Donat which crowns the peak, and from the former Capuchin Monastery, now a military hospital. Arlon was taken and burned by the Duke of Guise in 1558, and was re-fortified in the seventeenth century by Vauban, whose works did great damage to the old Roman walls, the foundations of which were almost as sound as in the days they were laid. Arlon has a good Provincial Museum containing many Roman antiquities found on the site of the town, and in the immediate neighbourhood. The region round about has many picturesque and flourishing villages for example Etalle, St. Léger, Athus, and Messancy; and there are at Clairefontaine some interesting

ruins of the Cistercian Abbey, founded in 1216 by a pious Countess of Luxembourg.

A few miles south west of Arlon there lies at Virton another Roman station, and in this part of the Ardennes is Florenville, perched high on a table land rising from a plain watered by the winding Semois. The town dates from the twelfth century, and is most noted, perhaps, for the width of its streets, and an immense square quite out of character and size with the number of its inhabitants. Chiny is a charming village with a ruined castle and shut in by exten-

Arlon. A staircase.

Arlon. The Calvary.

Arlon. Church doors.

sive woods ; while at Orval, on the south verge of the great forest of the same name, one has the ruins of a great Benedictine Abbey. Anciently the Monastery formed an enclosure of 52 acres in extent, and owned upwards of 300 villages, hamlets, and farms. It stands in a narrow lonely dell close to the French frontier, and is built on terraces, on one of the highest of which is an interesting Romanesque Chapel, while amidst the conventual buildings is the church rebuilt in the sixteenth and seventeenth centuries.

Bouillon everyone should see, for it is extraordinarily attractive, and has an air of antiquity. Its

Arlon. The new Church.

Ruins of the Abbey of Orval.

origin dates from the Frankish period of history, when, it is said, a few fishermen built their dwellings under the rocky, tree-clad hillside by the Semois, and thus laid the foundations of this tiny picturesque town. It was formerly the seat of a Dukedom in the Ardennes, and lies in the valley under the rocky ridge, on which are still to be seen the well-preserved remains of the Castle of Godfrey de Bouillon, the leader of the first Crusade. The town, skirting both banks of the river is connected by two bridges, and the stream forms a loop almost encircling the castle, from the walls of which there are beautiful views of the winding valley and well-wooded heights.

The grim, ruined castle, now a great pile of grey walls, in the crevices of which grow wild wallflowers, yellow snap-dragon, valerian, ivy, and even tiny trees, the silvery Semois, and the beautiful woods, which form a dark green background, make a charming picture and, indeed, one of the most delightful scenes in Belgium. Probably the castle dates from the seventh century, and in the tenth and eleventh centuries the family of the former holders took the titles of Dukes of Lower Lorraine and Bouillon. All these bore the name of Godfrey or Godefroy, the fifth of whom was the great Crusader. On September 3rd 1870 Napoléon III,

View of the Ruins of the Abbey of Orval.

a prisoner after the *débâcle* at Sedan, was brought to Bouillon on his road to Germany, and the room he occupied is still shown in the Hôtel de la Poste.

Bouillon makes an excellent holiday centre, and there are charming excursions towards Cordemois, which lies in the deep hollow of the valley where stretches a fine sheet of water. In this delightful spot is the Trappist Monastery of Cordemois reached by narrow and rocky paths winding through the woods and along the riverside. In front of the Monastery are vast grassy meadows, which slope to the foot of the opposite hills, through which the winding Semois threads its way like a silver ribbon.

Houffalize, more than a thousand feet above sea level, is the capital of the upper valley of the Ourthe, and is a finely situated summer resort. The parish church contains memorial slabs of the founder, Thierry, dating from 1243 with sculpture in high relief. St. Hubert with its forest is a rather interesting little place, with a small twelfth century Parish Church, and a very striking Abbey church of the early sixteenth century, which is seen from a great distance owing to its elevated position. St. Hubert is a great place for pilgrimages, and many miraculous cures are claimed for the saint's stole, which is preserved, with other relics, in the chapel of " The Apostle of the Ardennes. "

The river near Bouillon.

One comes to Laroche in a charming sweep of the Ourthe Valley amid lovely scenery that has doubtless had much to do with the fact that almost every house in the little town during the summer months is turned into a " dépendance" of the few quaint old hotels, for

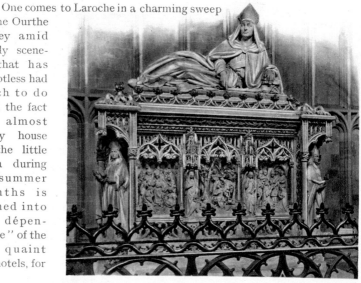

Bouillon. Tomb of St. Hubert.

Bouillon. View on the Semois.

Bouillon. Crypt of Church of St. Hubert.

the purpose of coping with the increasing number of visitors. The glory of Laroche lies chiefly in its fine surroundings, which include beautiful scenery of valley and rocky height, while the town itself, built on the river level at the end of the spurs of several hills and dominated by its ruined castle, is rendered all the more picturesque from

Detail of tomb of St. Hubert.

the fact that it is three parts encircled by a sharp bend of the Ourthe.

Durbuy is not only a picturesque old town, also on the tortuous windings of the Ourthe, but is the smallest township in Belgium, possessing a stately castle placed on a rocky eminence hard by. The chief street passes the foot of the castle, which in 1638 was partly destroyed but has been restored, and is still owned by the family of the Dukes d'Ursel into whose possession it came in the fifteenth century. The old bridge which spans the river is said to have been the only stone bridge on the Ourthe at the beginning of the nineteenth century.

To describe in detail the other numerous beauty spots, and picturesque little villages and towns that lie scattered through

Bouillon. Church of St. Hubert.

the delightful region of the Ardennes is beyond the scope of the present volume. There is, however, much in the variety of the scenery to tempt the traveller with time to spare more fully to explore this region of high plateaux, dense woodlands, charming valleys and pleasant streams.

It is along the white roads, which stretch across these moors, that the traveller reaches the highest points in Belgium, where are summits far higher than would be imagined by the vast majority of those who visit Belgium. The roads are lined here and there by pines, and as one passes along them it is through thickets of oaks and beeches, and past vast stretches of peaty soil.

This region of the high plateaux is an interesting one, and picturesque in a rather grim and severe manner. Here one sees solitary cottages set amid clumps of larches; low built houses with heavy slate roofs, made to withstand the winter gales which sweep over them. And here and there evidences of cultivation in the shape of small patches of rye and oats which indicate by their sparseness the difficulty they have to grow at all in such soil and on such wind-swept heights.

And as a contrast one has the romantic portion of the Ardennes with windmills, many of them ancient; hump-backed bridges, spanning purling streams; ruins of great feudal castles; villages and towns with crooked streets, conforming to the run of the ground; and picturesque peasants, the woman coming along the roads with baskets strapped to their backs.

These are things and beauties to discover for oneself, and they are well worth while.

View of Laroche.

Namur. View from the Citadel.

CHAPTER VI

—

Namur and down the Meuse to Dinant and Givet. The Southern Ardennes and the Grottoes of Han

The Meuse jade-green, or the colour of chrysoprase, flows placidly past Namur, a pleasant town, long famous for its cutlery, stretching along some distance on both banks of the river which is here spanned by the ancient Pont de Jambes of nine arches connecting Namur with the suburb of Jambes not far from the point where the canalised Sambre, which puts Charleroi and Mons in touch with the Meuse, joins the greater stream. There are delightful open spaces in Namur, many picturesque corners, and some quaint survivals to intrigue the artistic spirit in the wayfarer.

In summertime, too, the streets are made all the brighter by hanging baskets of flowers filled with lobelias, nasturtiums, pink-flowered ivy-leaved geraniums, and other plants which give a pleasant note of colour, and make the streets look as though perpetually en fête.

There are the charmingly laid out public walks and paths along the slopes of the old Ramparts environing the ancient fortress which frowns down upon the town. And then there is the pretty Park Marie-Louise, with its picturesque sheet of ornamental water, and well-shaded walks at the end of the tree-planted Boulevard de la Sambre, and adjoining the Avenue d'Omalius. From the Boulevard and the Park delightful views are obtainable across the river of the citadel, which occupies approximately the site of the fortress-dwelling of the ancient Counts of Namur. The latter was replaced towards the close of the seventeenth century by a strong fortress, the work of Cahorn, the famous Dutch engineer, who was the French Vauban's most formidable rival. In 1695 William of Orange captured it, and lovers of Sterne will recall that an account of this appears in " Tristram Shandy ", the hero being Uncle Toby.

Some of the charm of Namur is certainly derived from the picturesque situation of that portion of the town which lies thickly built on either side of the Sambre, from where it enters the Meuse at the Port de Grognon, for a considerable distance up the valley, especially along the Chemin de

The Meuse at Namur.

View of Namur and the Meuse.

Halage. Many of the houses are delightfully irregular as to their architecture, and the water rushing over the lock gates flecking the stream
with foam, and the barges passing on their way from Charleroi and Mons
into the Meuse make many pictures for artist and photographer alike.

Namur, too, has a distinctly friendly atmosphere; that intangible
quality which one must experience to realise. Most of the interesting
churches, of which several are fine examples of various schools of ecclesiastical architecture, are grouped somewhat closely together in the centre
of the city. Of them, that of St. Loup is the most interesting. Erected in
the Baroque style of the second quarter of the seventeenth century, it
possesses an imposing façade. The interior is spacious, and the roof is
supported by twelve red marble Doric colums. The choir strikes one as
somewhat flamboyant on account of the large amount of coloured marble
used in its ornamentation, and the ceilings are covered with rather heavily
conceived stucco ornamentation. Of special interest, however, are the
wonderfully carved confessionals, which for elaboration almost rival
those of Notre Dame, Antwerp, and St. Gudule, Brussels.

The Cathedral, which is dedicated to St. Aubin, or St. Alban, built
on the site of a very much earlier church, is an imposing but, on closer

Churches of St. Paul and St. Jean from the terrace.

acquaintance, somewhat disappointing building in brick. The present church was built during the sixteen years elapsing between 1751 and 1767 by the well-known Italian architect Pizzoni of Milan. Of the older church only the isolated belfry remains. The interior is impressive, and strikes one as being well proportioned; and the choir screen should be noted

Namur. The way to the Citadel.

from the fact that it was anciently in the Abbaye de Gembloux, founded in 922 by St. Wicbert, or Guibert, situated about a dozen miles north west of Namur. The wooden pulpit of the Cathedral is the work of Karel Hendrick Geerts, of Antwerp. The subject is " The Madon-

Namur. The Entrance to the Citadel.

Confessionals in the Church of St. Loup.

na protecting the City of Namur. " In the Treasury of the church is a famous and very interesting golden and jewelled crown of the thirteenth century, once belonging to Philip II, Count of Namur; and also a curious statuette of St. Blaise, dating from the early part of the fourteenth century.

The town belfry, which of old played so important a part in history, stands a little to the north of the Hôtel de Ville, and was built towards the close of the fourteenth century, and re-built two hundred years later.

The ancient "Boucherie", erected in 1588, one of the

oldest buildings surviving, standing in a narrow street close to the border of the river near one of the bridges spanning the Sambre, is now an Archaelogical Museum of considerable value, containing a very large and varied collection of antiquities chiefly relating to the Province of Namur. Indeed, it is well worth seeing, as it is claimed for it that it is the most complete collection of local Archaeology in Belgium, and some authorities even say in Europe.

Judging from the outside of the building one would not for a moment expect to find such treasures as are discoverable in these ancient and well-arranged rooms,

Carving in St. Antoine.

where skulls from the caverns of Marché-les-Dames, some of them possibly of pre-historic men; articles of the Stone Age from Linciaux, Sclaigneaux and Hastedon; bronzes from Ciney, Jambes, and Franchimont; ante-Roman and Frankish remains, pottery, specimens of fifteenth century glass, shrines, figures of saints from ancient churches, axes, from Eprave; and Belgic-Roman antiquities found at Namur, Anthée, Wancennes, Flavion, and other places, and many objects taken from ancient tombs and burying places of the fifth century onwards have been assembled together. There is an intensely interesting eleventh or twelfth century sarcophagus brought from a church at Hastière, down the Meuse just below Dinant, and several interesting pictures, and other Art treasures.

The most picturesque of the old houses in Namur are to be found along the left bank of the Sambre, and in the narrow streets which lead

Panel of the Confessionals in St. Loup.

from it back into the centre of the town. But there alas ! on a recent visit we found several missing from pre-War times, doubtless destroyed during the burnings of houses in which the Germans indulged so freely.

On the Sambre are to be seen many gaily painted barges, and interesting scenes of the life of the barge dwellers, numbers of whom spend the greater part of their existence on the canals and rivers of Belgium.

Namur. View of the Pont de Jambes.

Travellers who can do so should certainly proceed up the Meuse valley to Dinant or further, by car, cycle, or on foot; for only in this way can the beauty of the river and its scenery be adequately appreciated, and some of the little valleys, so charming in their verdure and made additionally picturesque by pleasant streams and tiny waterfalls, be explored. All the way to Givet are delightful, quaint, and tiny villages placed either on the river bank or clinging to the skirts of rocky gorges, and often sheltered by wooded crags. The comparatively narrow strip of land which here and there intervenes between the river and the road is beautifully cultivated, and its apple and cherry trees in springtime are a sheer delight, making the countryside exquisite, indeed.

The left bank is the best to travel. There is a good road for motorists, but pedestrians and cyclists have the pull of these in that they can go along the towpath, instead of following the main roads, and thus see many picturesque groups of *blanchisseuses* industriously washing and rinsing their huge piles of linen at the various cobbled slipways constructed for the purpose along the banks, or carrying on their operations from roughly made, though doubtless serviceable, punts.

The anglers of the Meuse are also a distinct feature. They are of all ages and of both sexes. Ones sees the urchins of Pairelle, Wépion, or Godinne with bean poles, lines of cotton, and a bent pin for a hook; the " sporting " man from Namur, dressed for the part, with best steel core fly rod and tackle, creel, landing net, campstool, etc; priests, who have come out of a monastery or presbytery hard by, who, by their attitude and intentness on the sport, inevitably remind one of the picture entitled " To-morrow will be Friday ".

All the way to Dinant, on both banks of the river there are some beautiful and delightfully placed modern châteaux, mostly the property of merchant princes of Namur and Brussels, and of other large towns. The natural scenery of wooded heights, rocks, and river is wonderfully varied when one remembers the comparatively confined area, and the short distance of some twenty miles which separates Namur from Dinant.

From Profondeville onwards to Rivière, the road is charmingly picturesque, and the river equally so. Rocky heights shut one in for a mile or so, and then comes a break with narrow green fields and grassy slopes stretching down to the Meuse on one hand, and away to the hills on the other. Then after a sharp bend one sees on the opposite bank the quaint old Seigneurie of Godinne, half-château, half-farm, with its feet literally in the water, white-walled, spired, and with its roofs and gables covered

The Meuse towards Rouillon.

with grey blue slates, throwing reflections in the evening light half-across the placidly flowing river. This beautiful old building, so typical of many which once adorned this stretch of the Meuse valley, is environed on its northern side by trees, and with its walls mellowed by age, river mists and storms, has a village church, dating from the sixteenth century, adjoining it built in the same style of architecture. It was once a portion of the patrimony of the well-known Du Mesnil family.

Less than a mile further on the road to Dinant, set in yet another bend of the winding river lies pretty little Rouillon clinging to the flank of a steep hill with its picturesque Château of Hestroy. Almost mid-way between here and Hun is the huge limestone rock overhanging the river known in the *patois* of the district as the Roche aux Chauwes or Crows' Rock, though the crows are in reality, as we found, jackdaws. The rock towers high above the road, riven into gullies and crevasses by the action of the weather through long ages, and pierced with hundreds of cavities in which the jackdaws from time immemorial have nested, making the air resound with their hoarse and shrill screaming which is weird enough to frighten nervous people after dusk. This rock and its generations of feather-ed inhabitants is the subject of a well-known legend called "The Fairy and the Troubadour" told by De Nimal in his "Légendes de la Meuse."

The Meuse near Rouillon.

View of Dinant.

Just above Godinne and Rouillon on the right bank of the river lies Yvoir at the mouth of the pretty little river Bocq. It is a delightfully picturesque village in which one seems to breathe the atmosphere of a by-gone age, and remembers the story of the four sons of Aymon who were contemporaries of Charlemagne, and to whom tradition ascribes the foundation of the great fortress. Of all this glory and romance of the past days and of the castle there remains but a memory, and the broken fragments of towers and galleries crumbling bit by bit under the influences of the forces of nature and of time. But there is a delightful little waterfall at Yvoir, and several picturesque mills at different points along the streams.

The Meuse near Yvoir is particularly picturesque, and though extensive quarrying goes on in the valley the beauty of it is not thereby greatly spoiled. A little to the south of Yvoir, on a lofty rock known as the Rocher de Champalle stand the ruins of the ancient fortress of Poilvache, which was destroyed by the French in 1554, and from the avenue leading up to it one gets a beautiful glimpse of the Meuse through the pine trees. At this point, as is so often the case in its upper reaches, the river seems almost to reproduce in miniature some of the beauties of the Rhine above Coblenz, and one has views of near by and distant wooded hills and picturesque townlets with the river winding its way in broad curves through the main valley.

In the immediate vicinity is the interesting and picturesque château of Crévecour.

Dinant and the Citadel.

The legend of Crévecour, is that in 1554, after Henry II of France had seized and sacked the place, three beautiful women, left as the only survivors after the massacre of the garrison, threw themselves, in sight of the besiegers, from the summit of one of the towers of the château, and were dashed to pieces on the rocks beneath. Their wraiths were for many years said to haunt the spot below the battlements where they met their deaths.

Bouvignes is a delightful little village, just on the outskirts of Dinant, once an important place indulging in frequent feuds and disputes with its big neighbour, but now only a shadow of its former self, though one of the most interesting and ancient places in this part of the Meuse Valley. One has some traces left of its former greatness in fragments of architecture, and here and there an ancient house, though alas ! several of the most important were burnt by the Germans during the War. There still

Dinant. The Roche à Bayard.

survives, however, on the Market Place the old sixteenth century Maison du Bailliage or Bailliff's House, one of the most remarkable in the Meuse Valley.

One of the most charming views of Dinant, sufficiently distant to obliterate at least some of the traces of the ravages of war, is obtained from the top of the Grotte du Trou-Chabeau, from whence one sees the beautiful river flowing on towards the ancient town, with the huge "Gibraltar" rock of the latter towering above the streets which have been rebuilt and seem to cling to the rocky gorge through which the river flows as though

A tugboat on the Meuse.

fearing to slip into its jade green waters.

Dinant is reached on the Bouvignes side of the river by a tree-environed road, in places elevated a considerable height above the water. Right opposite Bouvignes is the little river Leffe tumbling into the greater stream through a rocky and narrow valley up which are many beauty spots, and some delightful water mills.

The first real view one gets of Dinant, which largely rebuilt still bears many scars

The Roche à Bayard, near Dinant.

of the War, is through a gap in the trees and foliage which skirt the river side the last mile or so of the road, and seen at sundown this peep of the ancient and much suffering town is, indeed, beautiful and charming.

Dinant is by many authorities believed to date from Roman times. Its first name was Arche, the one by which it is now-a-days known having been bestowed upon it much later.

There are several theories regarding the derivation of the name of the town. That old and gossipy chronicler Jean D'Outremeuse gives the origin in a charming legend which is, briefly, as follows : — " Long ages ago St. Materne, the Apostle of the Ardennes, who was also Bishop of Tongres, came one day to the town whilst on an episcopal visitation or pilgrimage, and when walking in the streets saw an idol which the townsfolk had set up, and called Nam. Pointing to the figure the Saint exclaimed " Dis, or Dic Nam, pourquoi te tiens-tu ici " (literally " Tell me, Nam, why thou art found or set up here "). The inhabitants, the chronicler goes on to say, not hearing the whole of the Saint's remarks, but only the two first words, called their town forthwith Dinant. Other writers are of the opinion that the name was derived from Diane or Diana, and that the statue the Saint saw was one raised to the latter.

Dinant in past centuries has seen many vicissitudes, and during the Middle Ages it was frequently attacked, on several occasions by the Burgundians. In addition it was apparently at constant feud with Bouvignes, then " a place of strength and renown, capable of putting not less than 15,000 fighting men in the field. " In 1466 the Dinantais aroused the anger of Phillippe le Bon, Duke of Burgundy, who marched against the town in company with his son, afterwards known as Charles the Bold.

A few years later the Dinantais, hearing that the Burgundians had been heavily defeated by the people of Liége, marched towards Bouvignes with an effigy of the Duke's son Charles, Count of Charolais, swinging

Dinant. The new town.

between a gallows, " which they showed, " we are told " with many insults, to their enemies of Bouvignes ".

The Dinantais, however, had been misinformed. It was the people of Liége and not the Burgundians who had suffered defeat. And the Burgundians were at that moment marching to attack Dinant, and to avenge the insult to their Duke's heir. At the head of 30,000 men the Duke took up his quarters at the Abbey of Leffe, invested Dinant and ultimately captured the town. The place was sacked, and only the priests, women and children were spared, and these were deported to Liége. No less than 800 of the men were made prisoners, marched to Bouvignes, and there thrown into the river and drowned. There were many such cruel tragedies enacted in the Middle Ages.

Dinant viewed from across the water has a strangely curious and attenuated look. The lofty limestone cliffs, crowned by trees, and with ferns and lichen beautifying their face, at the back of the thin rows of new looking buildings, and towering high above the picturesque irregular roofs and chimney stacks, create an impression upon the beholder of endeavouring to thrust the houses from a precarious footing into the jade-coloured river itself.

Little remained save the bare walls of the ancient thirteenth century church of Notre Dame after destruction by the Germans in August 1914, and nothing of its once famous mosque-like, bulbous spire. The restored church

Bouvignes. The Church.

stands close against the rocky face of the Citadel, upon the site of the original building. It was formerly one of the most interesting churches in the Meuse Valley. The Baptistry on the right of the nave, with an ancient font, probably belonged to the Roman church which preceded the thirteenth century building. Behind the High Altar is a much more ancient one dedicated to Perpetuo, who was Bishop of Tongres.

Quite close to the church is a stone staircase of 408 steps by which one reaches the Citadel, where there is a museum containing

Anseremme and the River Lesse.

some souvenirs both of Waterloo and Sedan, and the reputed carriage of Madame de Maintenon, who is believed to have stayed at Dinant with Louis XIV, during the siege of Namur in 1692. It is well worth the climb to obtain the beautiful and widely stretching views one has of the valley of the Meuse extending from Bouvignes to Anseremme, and of the picturesque town below the great cliffs.

There is a pleasant road to Givet either along the right or the left bank, the latter is the more direct, and we fancy most usually taken. But it is worth while to go about a mile along the right bank of the river by way of the Rue Grande, and through the suburb of Les Rivages to see the famous Roche à Bayard. It is an extraordinary and imposing mass, which was pierced in 1698 to permit the baggage train of the French army, containing loot which filled 1600 vehicles requisitioned in the district, to pass. It is 180 feet in height, rising close to the banks of the river, and is some 50 feet wide at its base. It is here, the legend tells us, that the horse of the " Quatre Fils d'Aymon " named Bayard, which gives the rock its name, when pursued by Charlemagne jumped from the top of the heights into the Meuse. The rock, so the legend states, bore the impress of the horse's hoofs in the stone. Along the left bank of the river as far as Givet one has not only a picturesque and excellent road to follow, but some very pretty villages to pass through.

Anseremme is one of the prettiest, a great resort of artists, near the mouth of the Lesse and its charmingly wooded valley, and lies on the right bank of the river with a picturesque old Priory resting on an elbow of peaceful meadowland thrust out into the still waters of the Meuse, and forming a great contrast to the high rocky cliffs on the left

Rocky cliffs on the Meuse.

bank. The old monkish habitation forms a peaceful-looking oasis amid the grander scenery of the river above and below it.

One soon comes to Freyr resting on a beautiful stretch of the valley, and at this point, at the back of the little town, the slopes are less precipitous, and come gently down from the uplands clothed in dense woods, which extend to the flat meadows bordering the river, though tree-felling has in places somewhat spoiled them. The fine and stately Château de Freyr, of the seventeenth century, has a beautiful setting amid the varied greens of rich woodlands. The Gardens of the Château are said to have been laid out by Le Nôtre, and to have been modelled on those at Versailles. The treaty of Freyr, between Louis XIV of France and the imbecile Charles II of Spain was signed in the Château, on which occasion, it is said, coffee was served for the first time ceremoniously in Belgium.

The Lomme near Rochefort.

On the opposite shore to the village are great rocks consisting of huge masses and many " needles ", providing an excellent examples of the rugged scenery through which the Ardennes rivers make their way. These rocks rise in grotesque shapes precipitously out of the water to a great height, forming a bold promontory where the river sweeps round. The beautiful Valley of the little Lesse provides scene after scene of the greatest beauty. Rock and wood, cavern and grotto, pool and cascade, succeed one another up the comparatively short span of its course, the most interesting reaches of which are between Rochefort and Anseremme.

Château de Walzin.

The scenery from Freyr to Waulsort ever increases in picturesqueness and grandeur. Shortly after leaving the former place one comes upon the fine Château of the Comte de Loubespin situated, as is that of Freyr, close to the road near a beautiful bend in the river.

Hastiere-Lavaux lies in an open space in the valley with a broad treeshaded tow path and Hastière-par-delà across the stream lies in another sharp and picturesque bend of the Meuse. All interested in fine churches should cross the river to the smaller village of Hastière-par-delà where there is a very fine Romanesque church formerly belonging to the Abbey founded in the tenth century, and containing some remarkable frescoes by Donnay, who is considered by many as a disciple of Puvis de Chavannes. The high rocks above the village are the Rochers de Tahaux containing several great caverns.

Thirteen miles further and one reaches the French frontier town of Givet which is a rather gloomy looking place and stands on both banks of the river at the end of a narrow strip of French territory which projects into Belgium. Charlemont lies on a steep rock 700 feet in height from which a fine panoramic view of the river is obtained. In the industrial quarter of the Petit-Givet stands the church of Notre Dame containing fine wood carvings.

No one who wishes to know the Southern Ardennes can miss seeing Rochefort on the Lomme, formerly the capital of the County of Ardennes. It is a delightful little town as yet scarcely spoiled by the modernising

The Valley of the Lesse near Walzin.

spirit which, unhappily, pervades so many Continental resorts, and does so much to destroy both old-time atmosphere and historic buildings. Though Rochefort is an old town it has few buildings of historic interest; and the modern Town Hall is larger and rather pretentious looking and, cannot be compared in any way with the many masterpieces of Flemish architecture of a similar character.

Rochefort is dominated by the picturesque ruins of the ancient fortress, which, built in the thirteenth century, sustained in its time several sieges by the Spaniards and the French. Formerly the castle was the property of the Count of Stolburg.

The old town is strangely quaint and picturesque, and attracts a number of artists, and one cannot, too, fail speedily to realize that the air is unusually bracing and health giving. The Loretto Chapel of the Virgin, which stands on the heights above the famous grotto, and is reached through a delightful avenue of sweet smelling lime trees, is much visited as a pilgrim-

Entrance to the Grottoes of Han.

age spot, and from it a most beautiful and extensive prospect of the valley and the town can be obtained.

The principal church is a quite modern building in the Romanesque style from plans by Cluysenaer, and was built a little more than half-a-century ago. Rochefort is chiefly famous for its wonderful grotto, the entrance to which is at the end of the Rue St. Hubert not far from the ancient Carmelite Convent, now a private residence. The chief caverns are the Salle de Sabat, which is said to be 300 feet in height, the Salle des Merveilles, the Val d'Enfer, and Les Arcades.

Close to Rochefort stand the ruins of the famous Abbey of St. Remy, of recent years restored by the Benedictine monks. It was here that the Counts of Rochefort were buried. The handsome gateway and large courtyard belonged to the original building, very little else of which still remains.

The exploration of the delightful Valley of the Lesse is easily undertaken from Rochefort. It is rich in historic châteaux, and ancient strongholds. One of the most famous and romantically situated is that of Walzin, standing on an isolated rock which falls sheer down to the river at its foot. It is more easily approached from the cliffs behind than one would imagine, but seen from several points appears only capable of being reached by birds or aeroplanes. A fine view of the castle, which has been largely rebuilt in modern times, is obtained from the road, or the meadows across the stream. Formerly it was a stronghold of the de la Marck family of which the famous " Wild Boar of the Ardennes " was a member.

In this district are also to be seen the beautifully situated châteaux of Cergnon, Villiers, and Jamblines, these forming a really regal domain, which is the property of King Albert. The woodlands surrounding them are well stocked with game and the rivers with fish of all kinds. The scenery in the immediate neighbourhood is exceedingly beautiful, for Walzin is unspoiled and its sylvan beauties of infinite variety.

Hereabouts, at the feet of wild rocks, lie quiet meadows and still pools, while above these summit succeeds summit across this tiny land of smiling fertility living its peaceful life on the borders of its pleasant river. The Lesse is a stream of great variety, sometimes turbulent and broken by rapids, but at Walzin there is a quiet, pretty reach of wonderful clearness. A little ferry boat is drawn across by the help of a wire stretched over the stream, and not far away is the old mill, close to the quaint station of the little

The Lesse at Han.

The Exit from the Grottoes of Han.

railway that climbs unobtrusively up the valley. In this rugged district the people are few and the villages tiny, and even Walzin, one of the

The subterranean river Lesse.

best known and most accessible as well as most beautiful, has so few houses that it scarcely deserves the description of a village.

Only a few miles away lies Han-sur-Lesse, situated nearly 600 feet above sea level, and world-famous for its caverns or grottoes. These were discovered in the middle of the eighteenth century, and have been well known since the year 1771. The Hanais are fully alive to the value of the natural phenomen which has brought fame on their tiny village, and in the tourist season they reap a golden harvest from the visitors who flock to the spot. The grottoes are on so extensive a scale that they are reputed, how far with truth

The Lesse at Han.

Landscape in the Ardennes.

we cannot say, to be very little smaller in extent than the famous Caves of Kentucky in America. An elaborate system of lighting by electricity has been installed. The entrance to the grottoes is half-a-mile above the village itself, and the series of caverns form an immense natural cavity in the limestone rock. The entrance is by the Trou de Salpêtre, and one finds oneself almost at once in the first of the wonderful caverns or galleries. Among the principal caves which may be mentioned are the Salle de Scarabées, Tente Royale, the Salles Mosquée, Merveilleuse, and Alhambra, and the dainty Boudoir de Proserpine. The first really beautiful cave of stalagmites is known as La Grenouille. The corridor or Passage Collette, leads to the Salle Vigneron, named after a famous guide who years ago made many discoveries in the various caverns. The petrifactions of the Salle du Précipice are among the most remarkable of any in the Grotto, although the Salle des Mamelons, with its huge rounded boss-like stalagmites rising from the floor, which gives the cavern its name, and fairy-like stalactites depending from the roof is singularly beautiful. The Salle du Trophée which is nearly 70 feet in height with concretions that give the walls in places the appearance of being covered with the richest of shining draperies is very beautiful.

In the Valley of Han.

In the Salle de la Cascade one has a marvellous effect, as though a waterfall had suddenly become frozen. But it is not until the Gallerie Lannoy has been visited that the most wonderful and famous portion of the Grotto of Han is entered. In the Caverns poetically named Le Fragment, La Tiare, and Le Tonneau des Danaïdes, one sees the wonderful beauty of the stalagmites and stalactites fully exhibited. From the walls and ceilings and floors the glittering masses of pendant and uprising concretions flash back the rays of light, and one can almost imagine oneself in some fairy palace. There are several other caverns before one reaches the wonderful Salle des Draperies, where the tour ends, and the embarkation at the Passage du Diable on the subterranean river takes place.

Then, when the thunderous echoes of the cannon, which is fired, have died away after reverberating from cavern to cavern, roof to roof, and corner to corner, the passage from the profundity of night of the underworld to the sunshine of the outer commences. The light, at first so soft and diffused, which one perceives ahead as the boat takes its course increases gradually in refulgence, and the sight of nature bathed in sunlight, which at length bursts upon one's vision, is fairy-like and unspeakably beautiful. It is, perhaps, from its appeal to the love of light and life which actuates everyone, the most charming sight of all connected with this marvellous underworld of the grottoes of Han. It is certainly the most vivid impression that one receives and retains. From the light thrown fitfully back from the shining stalactites and stalagmites one glides out into a world of calm water, green trees clothing the hillside, and the ambient sunshine of a summer's day.

Pleasant weeks can be spent in exploring the beautiful valleys and natural beauties of this portion of the Ardennes, including the small town of Jemelle, where two little tributaries of the Lesse meet, and in the neighbourhood of which is scenery of great ruggedness and charm.

Another little village worth visiting is Eprave where the Lomme returns to the surface, after its long underground journey from Rochefort, to turn the old mill wheels before it falls in to the Lesse.

So thus has one seen the portion of Belgium which is less known to the general tourist and holiday maker, with its ancient cities, pleasant and picturesque towns, two great rivers, lesser streams, and romantic valleys, and beautiful scenery; all of which combine to leave an ineffaceable impression of charm and delight.

The Ourthe at Comblain.

The Road to Rochefort near St. Hubert.

INDEX

Semois, 121-122-123-126-127-129.
Spa, 91-94-97-98-99-100-101-102-103-104-106-110-111.
Spaloumont, 102.
Stavelot, 106-107-112.
Steen, 10-14-15-17-38-39.
Sure, 122.

T

Teniers, David, 12-23-30-58-83.
Terburg, Gerard, 30.
Tête de Flandre, 13-38-40.
Theux, 94-96.
Thierry, 127.
Tilff, 108.
Titian, 30.
Tongerlo, Abbey of, 32.
Tongres, 74-100-147.
Trois-Ponts, 107.

V

Van der Weyden, Roger, 63.

Van Dyck, 12-47-58.
Van Orley, B., 12-30.
Vaux-sous-Chèvremont, 91.
Verhaghen, 66.
Verviers, 91-106.
Vesdre, 74-89-91-92-94-110.
Virton, 123.
Vriendt, Frans de, 30.

W

Wache, 111-112.
Walzin, 135-153-154-156.
Wancennes, 139.
Waulsort, 152.
Wépion, 141.
William de la Marck, 108.
William of Orange, 134.

Y

Ypres, 70.
Yvoir, 143.